THE
MOTIVATION
CODE

THE MOTIVATION CODE

*Discover the Hidden Forces
That Drive Your Best Work*

Todd Henry

with Rod Penner, Todd W. Hall, PhD,
and Joshua Miller, PhD

PRUVIO PRESS

PRUVIO PRESS

Copyright © 2020 by Pruvio, LLC

PRUVIO™, THE MOTIVATION CODE™, and MCODE™
are trademarks of Pruvio, LLC.
SIMA® is a registered trademark of Sima II, LLC.
Book design by Daniel Lagin

*To Arthur Miller Jr.,
who laid the foundation for Motivation Code
with his pioneering work in SIMA,
and to all the practitioners who will use
Motivation Code to bless future generations.*

CONTENTS

Introduction — ix

PART I
WHAT DRIVES YOU? — 1

Chapter 1 **Unique Motivation Is the Missing Key** — 3

Chapter 2 **Discover Your Motivation Code** — 17

PART II
THE MOTIVATIONAL THEMES — 27

Chapter 3 **The Visionary Family** — 29

Chapter 4 **The Achiever Family** — 51

Chapter 5 **The Team Player Family** — 83

Chapter 6 **The Learner Family** — 113

Chapter 7 **The Optimizer Family** — 141

Chapter 8 **The Key Contributor Family** — 181

PART III
NOW WHAT? 215

Chapter 9 **Living Out Your Motivation** 217

Acknowledgments 229

Appendix A: **Additional Resources** 231

Appendix B: **Motivation Code's Technical Development and Validation** 233

Index 245

Introduction

MY STORY

ONE DAY, OUT OF THE BLUE, I RECEIVED AN EMAIL FROM MY FRIEND ROD Penner, who was a twenty-year veteran of a world-famous management consulting firm. I knew he'd left the organization years before, but wasn't certain what he'd been doing since.

"I'd like you to take a motivation assessment I've been working on."

As someone steeped in corporate training, research into collaboration and creativity, and all things trendy in business, I was nonplussed at the idea of having another set of letters to attach to myself. (I'm an INTP—you?) However, upon further urging by Rod, I decided to give it a go.

The next day, I breezed through the Motivation Code (MCODE) assessment that Rod and his team had developed, hit enter, and awaited Rod's response. He'd promised that he'd go over the results with me personally so I could better understand the work he'd dedicated the last several years of his life to. An email arrived with a report containing my results, and Rod and I scheduled time to discuss it.

I wasn't prepared for what happened next.

On our call, Rod explained to me the reasoning behind every life decision I've made, the areas where I struggle to find the drive needed to excel, and the common through-line connecting the high points of my personal and professional life. He offered a blueprint for understanding why certain tasks were exhilarating to me and why some were simple drudgery. Why I made certain decisions in my life other people have said were crazy. Why I've succeeded in some leadership roles and struggled in others. And, well, just about everything else I've ever lacked words to explain. In short, it was like Rod had been reading some secret transmission between my gut and my brain that determined my choices.

I was blown away.

Rod had identified my Motivation Code™, or the themes that drive deep satisfaction and engagement in my life and work, and the potential shadow sides of those motivations that explained many of the unproductive tendencies in my life.

I realized that Rod and the team he was working with were on to something much bigger than just a nice new framework to make people feel a little more engaged at the office. They had unlocked something deep and primal that—once understood—could radically change how people approach their work each day.

Later I learned that the Motivation Code assessment was the result of the work of an entire team of brilliant PhDs, researchers, and consultants. It was also founded upon decades of qualitative research on motivation, and over 100,000 interviews with executives, salespeople, teachers, clergy, artists, and people from nearly all walks of life about moments when they felt deeply gratified with an achievement. In fact, their research dates back to the early 1960s and is sourced in the work of Arthur Miller Jr., the founder of a company called SIMA.* Over many decades, Miller and his colleagues explored and mapped patterns related to motivation and engagement. This new team of researchers,

---

* More information about SIMA can be found at simainternational.com.

under the company name Pruvio,™* had taken Miller's work even further by developing a story-driven assessment that utilizes psychometric methods to determine motivational themes. Their key discovery is that if we can understand the commonalities within achievement stories that stick with us for decades, then we can unlock the unique "code" that drives behavior, life satisfaction, and excellent work.

This work on practical motivation is cutting-edge and takes to a new level what we've traditionally understood to be true about what drives human behavior and engagement. Rather than relying upon the traditional categories of "intrinsic" and "extrinsic" motivation, the Motivation Code framework recognizes—as leading psychologists and researchers have shown us in recent decades—that these types of motivation are not fully discrete, but instead interact with and modify one another. Motivation Code captures the unique and precise way that each individual is driven to achieve a specific kind of result. As you will see, understanding it has a number of practical benefits, from deeper engagement to better productivity to improved relationships.

In the following chapters, you will discover a concise and effective explanation of what drives you. If you commit to the process described in this book, you will gain deep understanding of the *why* behind your actions and decisions and acquire tactical insights for how to find greater satisfaction in your life and in your work.

This book will also change how you see the people on your team and how you organize and lead them through their work responsibilities. As I will share later, engaged teams are much more productive and collaborative, and significantly more likely to stick together through difficult seasons. Once you have insight into the motivations of your team members, you can guide them with much more precision because you will understand what makes them tick. You will also be better equipped to retain top talent because you will understand what really

---

* For more about Pruvio and our work, visit pruvio.com.

drives them, and know in which roles and team environments they are most likely to thrive. If you learn to speak directly to their unique motivations, you'll gain both their attention and their trust.

So, in short, this book will help you and those you lead to be more fulfilled and more productive, and to bring your unique contribution to the world every day.

One quick note: readers will notice that the authors occasionally use personal pronouns. Where "I" is used, it refers to me, Todd Henry. Where "we" is used, this refers to all four authors, myself included.

THE MOTIVATION CODE

PART I

WHAT DRIVES YOU?

Chapter One

UNIQUE MOTIVATION IS THE MISSING KEY

FRANK WAS AN ENGINEER FOR A LARGE PUBLIC AGENCY. HE'D BEEN DO-ing well in his previous department, where he did a lot of research, technical engineering work, and problem solving. But he'd recently moved to a new department. In his new position, he did less technical engineering and research work because his boss wanted him to handle more and more project management.

In this new role, Frank struggled to stay organized. He dreaded negotiating contracts with outside vendors. He didn't like working with all the details and regulations related to contracts and spreadsheets. As a result, he started avoiding some tasks, got behind in his work, resented taking work home when he had to, and generally wasn't performing well.

Frank didn't understand why he wasn't flourishing in his new department. On paper, he was perfect for the job. He had all the right skills and expertise needed to succeed. Still, he felt frustrated and demoralized. But, there were larger patterns playing out that Frank wasn't aware of. And these patterns play out in your life as well.

Think about a time when you felt on top of the world, or a moment of real accomplishment that stands out.

Maybe you landed a big client you'd been working on for months. Maybe you hit the game-winning shot that catapulted your team to the league championship. Maybe you helped a friend through an especially difficult situation and as they left, you thought, "Wow—that was amazing."

We all have memories of great achievements. But have you ever stopped to consider *why* those experiences were so meaningful? For instance, landing the client might have been about the rush of tackling an external challenge, gaining ownership over a new sales territory, or bringing order to another organization's processes. Hitting the shot might have been about the satisfaction of being a key contributor to the success of the team, shutting up the naysayers who said you would lose, or demonstrating mastery of the three-pointer. Helping a peer through a situation might have been about the joy of being there for someone else, influencing another's behavior, or sharing knowledge you'd recently learned.

Like Frank, we often gloss over the deeper patterns of behavior and emotion that define our most cherished experiences without bothering to examine what they might say about us. Who has time to look backward when there's so much to do? However, it's by paying attention to these patterns that we can discover what most engages us, what yields true satisfaction, and what drives us to work more deeply, live more richly, and produce the best work of our lives.

Eventually, Frank had had enough. He began working with a coach who helped him discover his Motivation Code. Through the Motivation Code assessment, Frank discovered that his top three motivational themes are:

- Evoke Recognition
- Demonstrate New Learning
- Achieve Potential

And just as important, his bottom two themes are:

- Bring to Completion
- Organize

Frank's Demonstrate New Learning motivation led him to naturally gravitate toward researching issues and then teaching his technical expertise to others, and his Achieve Potential theme drove him to identify the best possible solution to every problem. So doing this kind of work in his previous role, he was energized and performed at a very high level. Frank had a reputation in his company for being the go-to person when you had a complex engineering problem. But when it came to organizing and completing projects, these were at the bottom of his motivational themes, so it suddenly became clear why these new tasks completely drained him.

As Frank discussed his Motivation Code with his coach, he said it suddenly illuminated for him patterns in his life that had repeated over and over, but that he'd never been able to put into words. It provided a shortcut for understanding why certain tasks were energizing and others were simple drudgery. Once he understood these patterns, Frank was able to have a more meaningful discussion with his manager about his workload so they could shape his job in a way that leveraged the best of his abilities and motivations while allowing others to handle the responsibilities that completely drained him. He, and the entire organization, became more productive, engaged, and on target to hit their objectives.

MOTIVATION IS FELT BUT NOT ALWAYS UNDERSTOOD

Most of us are like Frank. We've never really stepped back to examine the patterns in those moments when our work is especially gratifying or engaging. We gloss over the deeper patterns of meaning and motivation in our life in order to move on to the next challenge.

You might think that the *why* behind those moments of deep satisfaction would be obvious, but in fact there is a lot going on beneath the surface that is not always apparent, not even to ourselves. This is because humans are story-making machines. We have a psychologically ingrained need to make sense of our experiences, mostly as a form of psychological or physical self-protection. Therefore, many of the reasons we give for why we do what we do are actually just stories that we use to justify our behavior, even if they aren't fully accurate about what really drives us.

Nineteenth-century psychoanalyst Ernest Jones first coined the term "rationalization" to describe the human need to explain inexplicable behavior after the fact. He wrote, "No one will admit that he ever deliberately performed an irrational act, and any act that might appear so is immediately justified by . . . providing a false explanation that has a plausible ring of rationality." Because of this dynamic, without some kind of external feedback mechanism to help identify noteworthy patterns in our behavior, it can be difficult to gain an objective read on why we actually make the choices we make, or why we find certain activities motivating or draining.*

The reality is, the *why* behind what drives us is very complex. For example, consider three people who are up for a promotion, all of whom covet the new role. Deep down, one person might be motivated to pursue the promotion because of the increased challenge associated with the role and the opportunity to tackle new and potentially overwhelming work. The second person might look at the managerial team they would be joining and be driven to become a part of something great. A third might see the promotion as an opportunity to finally have their say in the decisions of the organization and gain influence over the systems and processes they have taken issue with for a number of years.

---

* Ernest Jones, "Rationalization in Every-Day Life," *Journal of Abnormal Psychology* 3, no. 3 (1908): 161–69.

All three of these people might be pursuing the exact same role, but for very different reasons. However, if you were to ask them a few years down the line why they chose to seek that promotion, the story they would tell would likely be related to the external outcomes of their decision. For example, they might say, "I took the job to better provide for my family," or "I needed a change, and this seemed like a good opportunity," or "I wanted to stay in the same city so my kids wouldn't have to switch schools." To explain the reason for their action, they might backward-rationalize in light of whatever external benefits their choice resulted in. In other words, they would create a new story.

While these external reasons—increase in pay, nature of work, convenience of location—might be somewhat accurate, they're not comprehensive. To really comprehend the fullness of why we are driven to make certain decisions, we also need to understand how these external factors interplay with our unique inner drivers.

DEFINING MOTIVATION CODE

Each individual has a unique blend of motivations that drive behavior and a sense of engagement. We call this your Motivation Code. It explains why you are willing to dedicate hours to doing something others would despise, why you feel compelled to collaborate with a team *or* always desire to work alone, why recognition is high on your list of priorities *or* why praise doesn't matter at all as long as you are pleased with your work, why you make the same mistakes over and over, *or* why you always seem to experience conflict with your differently motivated peer, manager, or spouse.

Motivation Code is the unique, constant, unchanging behavioral drive that orients a person to achieve a distinct pattern of results.

Unique. Your Motivation Code is the distinct combination of motivational drivers that animate your best work and deepest sense of engagement. It is how your internal motivations uniquely respond to external circumstances. While motivation is typically described as being either intrinsic (internal, personal) or extrinsic (external, rewards based), these two types of motivation are not completely independent of each other. Instead, they interact, creating a complex blend of behavioral and emotional drivers. Your Motivation Code accounts for all of these intrinsic and extrinsic factors, and it is unique to you.

Constant. Your Motivation Code persists through success and failure, through challenging and easy tasks. It doesn't waver depending on the work you are engaged with. Instead, your experience of life and work is filtered through the lens of your Motivation Code.

Unchanging. Your Motivation Code tends to remain the same over long periods. What motivated you five years ago is likely to be the same thing that is driving you today.

Once you discover your Motivation Code, you are likely to see how it has driven many of your significant decisions and moments of gratifying achievement. It's like a key, missing piece of the puzzle that suddenly allows you to see the full picture. Before we dive deeper into how your Motivation Code influences you, let's dispel a few misunderstandings about the nature of motivation.

Misunderstandings About Motivation

Motivation is just about diligence or laziness. When we say that someone isn't motivated, it's often code for "that person is lazy." But that's not necessarily true. Though we all have moments of laziness or times when we're simply too worn out to be engaged, it may likely be because some activities require us to operate outside of our Motivation Code and are therefore naturally more draining.

For example, some of us would gladly work on a novel during our nights and weekends off, create a website to promote a charity drive, or volunteer to organize the office holiday party year after year, but the idea of sitting through one more quarterly strategy meeting makes us want to curl up in the fetal position. It's not that we're lazy or unwilling, it's just that some work is more energy draining than energy giving. We will do it, of course, but we're not *motivated* to.

Motivation is just about enjoying tasks. Most of us have to do things we don't want to do in order to achieve our objectives. However, those who are operating within their Motivation Code can find greater meaning and gratification in doing even the tasks they don't necessarily enjoy.

For example, filing paperwork is probably not on many people's list of enjoyable activities. However, for the person motivated to organize, the act of sequencing files and finding new ways of ordering information can be deeply gratifying. Similarly, for the person motivated by challenges, the bigger the better, cranking through as many files as possible can leave them craving an even loftier mountain to climb. Each person finds the work gratifying, but for very different reasons. Once they understand how, they can learn to activate their Motivation Code throughout their day, even for those tasks that don't seem exciting.

Motivation just naturally comes with "the perfect job." Many people jump from job to job throughout their career looking for the perfect fit that will fulfill them. But the truth is, chasing "the perfect job" is a fool's errand. All jobs have grueling elements, and if you leave a job the moment it becomes uninteresting or boring, you may never develop the expertise necessary to reach a level of true and lasting proficiency.

However, understanding your Motivation Code can help you identify the kinds of environments in which you are more *likely* to thrive, and those that might unnecessarily drain you. Just like Frank in the story above, understanding your Motivation Code can help you have a more meaningful conversation with your manager about your role and the areas where you are naturally driven and engaged.

WHAT MANAGERS HAVE TRIED

According to Gallup's 2017 *State of the American Workplace* report, a mere 33 percent of employees are engaged at work. Two thirds are disengaged, many of them actively.*

Here's another stat: 21 percent of employees strongly agree their performance is managed in a way that motivates them to do outstanding work. In other words, only about one fifth of employees feel their manager understands what makes them tick and routinely tries to stoke their fire. What a huge missed opportunity!

This isn't just about having more satisfied employees. It's about the very long-term viability of the business. The same report argues that there is a direct connection between higher engagement and the economic health of the organization, estimating that actively disengaged employees cost the United States $483 billion to $605 billion each year in lost productivity. On top of that, actively disengaged employees are almost twice as likely as engaged employees to seek new jobs. Higher turnover means more time and resources spent hiring, which means

---

* Gallup, www.gallup.com/workplace/238085/state-american-workplace-report-2017.aspx.

more hours dedicated to training and development, which results in a constant redefining of the team culture, and all of it has a trickle-down effect on the bottom line. This isn't because employees don't know what to do or aren't equipped to do it. It's simply because they're not being led in a way that engages them. They are simply not motivated.

Knowing that engaged employees are critical to a successful organization, companies have been trying to unlock the key to employee motivation for decades. There are a number of ways that managers have tried to animate their teams toward better productivity, with varying success.

Compensation and Praise

Pay raises, benefits, paid time off, and bonuses are often the go-to for rewarding good work. They're effective to some degree—everyone needs to pay the bills and care for their family—but while compensation can spur you to do something in the short term, it doesn't necessarily mean that you *want* to do it. Instead, you do what you have to do in order to "earn the carrot" and little else, making a compensation-based system of motivation most effective for getting employees to do the minimum necessary to receive the reward.

Not only does compensation fail to address our unique motivational needs, but these sorts of attempts to compel action can have a diminishing effect on long-term motivation. In 1971, professor of psychology at the University of Rochester Edward L. Deci, one of the cofounders of self-determination theory, conducted a study to determine whether external rewards in the form of money could affect intrinsic motivation. According to the study, "Results indicate that (a) when money was used as an external reward, intrinsic motivation tended to decrease; whereas (b) when verbal reinforcement and positive feedback were used, intrinsic motivation tended to increase." This was especially true when a participant was performing an enjoyable task in which they experienced a high degree of intrinsic motivation.*

This study showed that once external rewards "crowd out" intrinsic motivation, those extrinsic rewards must continue in order to motivate behavior. Once it's gone, the original intrinsic motivation does not return.

But what about verbal reinforcement, encouragement, and positive feedback, which are also extrinsic motivators? According to Deci's study, praise also contributed to an increase in intrinsic motivation, but only in the short term. Because constant feedback and encouragement are required to sustain performance under these conditions, this may not be the most optimal long-term solution to the motivation problem.

Flexibility and Perks

Many organizations attempt to motivate their employees by granting them greater flexibility, the freedom to work remotely, or more prestigious titles. Several are transitioning to remote working schedules as both a cost-saving measure and a way to provide better life balance for employees. (The irony, of course, is that the "balance" is often worse when work is always in the next room instead of a commute away.) Like compensation and praise, this form of motivation works to a certain point, but flexibility and perks won't always animate you to bring your best effort to a project. In fact, for those motivated to collaborate with others, or who derive their motivational energy from organizing teamwork, workplace flexibility might actually decrease their motivation.

None of the above methods, or many others that are attempted, are effective over long periods of time because, as we've discovered, they don't fully account for Motivation Code.

---

* Edward L. Deci, "Effects of Externally Mediated Rewards on Intrinsic Motivation," *Journal of Personality and Social Psychology* 18, no. 1 (1971): 105–15.

WHAT ACTUALLY WORKS

Imagine a series of lockers. You need to retrieve valuable items from inside them, but each one is closed and locked with a padlock. If you were willing to make a mess, you could smash the padlocks with a sledgehammer or destroy the lockers with a blowtorch. This would be a "brute force" method, and while it would grant you access to each of the lockers, it would certainly not be the most efficient way to open them. You could cause a lot of damage to yourself, the lockers, and their contents in the process. Also, think about all the energy you'd waste trying to smash open the lockers.

Because they don't know any other method, many managers resort to "brute force" or "one size fits all" approaches to motivate their teams. As we've learned, these might include incentives like pay, perks, titles, and promotions, but also unhealthy, fear-based behaviors such as harsh language, threats, and constant critical feedback. Just as opening the lockers with brute force can result in damage and wasted time, brute force motivation tactics can be largely inefficient because they don't speak to what truly mobilizes each individual. Also, as Deci demonstrated in his study, while effective at first, these brute force approaches lose their power over time.*

Now imagine that you've been given a list of the combinations to the padlocks. Wouldn't it be easier (and much neater) to open the padlocks using their proper codes? Of course it would. This method is precise and causes no damage. In the same way, understanding the unique Motivation Code of each team member is the key to unlocking engagement, and this results in significant benefits to team dynamics and, ultimately, your organization's bottom line.

---

* Deci, "Effects of Externally Mediated Rewards," 105–15.

Benefits of Managing with Motivation Code

Retention. Understanding what motivates the people on your team is critical to not only having an engaged and thriving workplace culture, but also to ensuring the economic viability of your company. Unmotivated employees will begrudgingly follow orders for a while, but they'll eventually seek better opportunities. On the other hand, those who develop and retain the best talent keep employees for years and years without wasting precious dollars on hiring and training.

Cohesion. Understanding the underlying motivations of team members can help you resolve common areas of conflict. For example, if you're having continuous power struggles over who gets to lead a project, it could be because several team members have a need to be at the center of the action. If there is a lot of blame shifting or a general lack of accountability, it may be because there aren't enough achievement-oriented people who find it necessary to advance the project. Does your team perform very well in the early stages but struggle to make progress once they hit a roadblock? This may be because you don't have any employees who are driven to complete projects, and instead your team is made up of visionaries who get excited about ideas but not about making those ideas happen.

Once you understand what motivates each member of your team, you'll begin to see why certain patterns of behavior play out over and over, and you'll understand how to fix them.

Momentum. Do you find that your team stalls later in the project, when it's time to deliver the final product? Or do they come on strong in the final stages, though they typically get off to a slow and painful start? Or do you find that conflict always seems to impede progress? This lack of momentum could be a result of the conflicting motivational drivers of team members. Once you begin to understand these patterns and how they affect your team's drive, you will be able to lead your team much more effectively.

BEFORE WE DIVE IN

Have you ever had a friend who hopped from cultural trend to cultural trend, always looking for the answer to their problems? "Wow—this book just changed my life," they might say. "No, wait . . . *this* book just changed my life."

You are about to go on a journey of self-discovery that is likely to change how you approach your life and work. Before you do, here are a few preliminary bits of advice to help you get the most out of what you'll learn in the chapters ahead:

> *Motivation is the foundation for personal development.* I've seen firsthand how an understanding of Motivation Code has transformed people's sense of self, catapulted positive career changes, and improved relationships with their direct reports, colleagues, and team members. But motivation alone is not enough: to produce your best work, you must leverage that motivation to develop your skills and expertise. Motivation is the foundational layer that supports your ability to pursue new levels of productivity and achievement.

> *Motivation has both a positive side and a shadow side.* As you'll see in the coming chapters, there are both positives and potential negatives that come with each motivation. Understanding your Motivation Code will help you look out for those instances in which you are tempted to behave badly at the expense of others: "Well, I can't help but steal the spotlight. I am, after all, motivated to Evoke Recognition."

> *Motivation is not a full description of you and your identity.* Humans are very complex, and motivation is only one aspect of who you are. And, please understand that with regard to Motivation Code, there are no good or bad motivations. Don't worry if you don't immediately

like (or agree with) what you discover through this process. Your Motivation Code is not intended to be worn like a name tag. It is meant to help you better understand why you are driven to achieve certain outcomes, and the unique opportunities that accompany those drives.

Chapter Two

DISCOVER YOUR MOTIVATION CODE

THROUGHOUT THE REST OF THIS BOOK, I WILL WALK YOU THROUGH A process to help you identify and activate your Motivation Code. First, you'll learn about the various motivational themes and families that comprise the Motivation Code framework. Then, I will share how you can take the free Motivation Code assessment (motivationcode.com/free) to determine your top motivations. Finally, I will offer some real-world advice about how to activate your newfound knowledge of Motivation Code in your life and work.

THE MOTIVATIONAL THEMES

Your Motivation Code is composed of your top three motivations, or motivational themes. Within the Motivation Code framework, there are twenty-seven distinct motivational themes:

1. Achieve Potential	10. Serve	19. Make It Work
2. Make an Impact	11. Influence Behavior	20. Develop
3. Experience the Ideal	12. Comprehend and Express	21. Establish
4. Meet the Challenge	13. Master	22. Evoke Recognition
5. Overcome	14. Demonstrate New Learning	23. Bring Control
6. Bring to Completion	15. Explore	24. Be Unique
7. Advance	16. Organize	25. Be Central
8. Collaborate	17. Make It Right	26. Gain Ownership
9. Make the Grade	18. Improve	27. Excel

Given the number of motivational themes and their possible combinations, it's easy to see why Motivation Code is so unique to the individual. There are 2,925 possible combinations of top three motivations, and 17,500 possible Motivation Codes. So while any two people might share a theme, it's unlikely that their top two would be the same, and having three themes in the same order would be even more implausible. For example, imagine two individuals who have Meet the Challenge as their primary motivational theme: they both love to climb mountains. But while the first person prefers to climb with others, because they have Collaborate as their secondary theme, the other, who has Master as their second strongest theme, prefers to climb on their own to perfect their technique.

This is an important point: *motivational themes modify one another.* So it's likely that two people who have a particular primary theme in their Motivation Code might acquire their motivational energy in a slightly different way, depending on what their other top motivations are. This means that Motivation Code is a very precise and personal way of describing what truly drives you.

The Motivational Families

Although each motivational theme has distinct attributes, there are some common characteristics across certain themes that group them together into what we call motivational families. For example, themes within the Visionary Family are generally about looking to the future. But each one gives off motivational energy in a very unique way. For this reason, it's important to focus on the individual themes, not families, when interpreting your Motivation Code. The families are simply a way of showing which themes share a little DNA.

Here are the motivational themes, grouped by families:

Visionary	Achiever	Team Player
1. Achieve Potential	4. Meet the Challenge	8. Collaborate
2. Make an Impact	5. Overcome	9. Make the Grade
3. Experience the Ideal	6. Bring to Completion	10. Serve
	7. Advance	11. Influence Behavior

Learner	Optimizer	Key Contributor
12. Comprehend and Express	16. Organize	22. Evoke Recognition
13. Master	17. Make It Right	23. Bring Control
14. Demonstrate New Learning	18. Improve	24. Be Unique
15. Explore	19. Make It Work	25. Be Central
	20. Develop	26. Gain Ownership
	21. Establish	27. Excel

COMPLETE THE MOTIVATION CODE ASSESSMENT

Now that you have a general understanding of themes and families, it's time to discover what makes you tick. To do this, you will take the free Motivation Code assessment (motivationcode.com/free), which is a story-based psychometric assessment designed to help you understand the common themes in your moments of deep satisfaction and great achievement.

Step One: Identify Your Achievement Stories

To begin the Motivation Code assessment, think of an achievement story: a moment in your life when you accomplished something meaningful. It doesn't matter if it was notable to others or if it had a big impact. The most important factor is that this accomplishment has remained in your memory for a while and in some way defines how you see yourself in the world.

An achievement story is made up of three parts:

1. Name an accomplishment that gave you deep satisfaction.
2. Describe what you actually did.
3. Explain what about the achievement was particularly enjoyable to you.

Below is an achievement story I used the first time I took the Motivation Code assessment.

> *Name an accomplishment that gave you deep satisfaction.* In my senior year of high school, I played varsity basketball and helped lead our team to an 18–5 season and a state ranking. In the previous two years, we'd had 0–21 and 2–19 seasons, so this was a huge turnaround and a tremendously gratifying experience.
> *Describe what you actually did.* After I came down with a serious illness in my sophomore year, the doctors told me I might never play basketball again. Despite losing sixty pounds and having to use a walker and cane for weeks, I was back in the gym after just six months. The following year, I made it back on the team and even scored a majority of the points.
> *Explain what about the achievement was particularly enjoyable to you.* Leading my basketball team to victory after being told I

might never play again showed me that hard work over a prolonged period can yield results. I learned that it's not where you start, but where you finish that matters.

You'll notice that my responses are not long or elaborate, but are specific and direct. This is the most important thing about relaying your achievement stories: to obtain the most accurate results from the assessment, be as precise in your responses as possible.

When completing the assessment, don't overthink which achievement stories you use. If a memory immediately pops to mind, take note of it: there's likely a reason for that. However, a good story tends to have a few particular qualities.

It's specific, concrete, and in the past. Your achievement story should not be a large, vague, general accomplishment ("Growing my awareness of geopolitics"), but something very specific that took place within a certain time frame and is now in the past ("I took a course in geopolitics at a local college and earned an A").

It's meaningful to you, even if no one else cares. Your achievement story might be long forgotten by others, but that doesn't matter. All that matters is that it sticks in your mind as a high point of personal (or team) accomplishment.

It's withstood the test of time. The best achievement stories are the ones that took place months and years, not days or weeks, ago and are still hanging around in your mind for a reason.

We recommend that you write down three full achievement stories before taking the Motivation Code assessment. First, this will allow you to identify some common threads that tie your stories together and might give you a bit of insight into what drives you. Also, by identifying multiple stories, you can start to see how your Motivation Code has shown up in various ways over time, and how it plays out differently depending on the circumstances.

> **Exercise (30 minutes)**
>
> 1. List five to seven possible achievement stories. Don't elaborate on them yet. Just list a few options.
> 2. Take a few moments to remember the three parts of an achievement story: name an accomplishment that gave you deep satisfaction, describe what you actually did, and explain what about the achievement was particularly enjoyable to you.
> 3. Select the three achievement stories that most resonate with you and represent moments of genuine fulfillment. Avoid choosing stories just for the sake of pleasing others—that doesn't matter. All that matters is that these moments mattered to you.
> 4. Write down your achievement stories following the three-part framework.

Step Two: Take the Assessment

Once you've written down your achievement stories, visit motivationcode.com/free to take the free Motivation Code assessment. It takes about thirty minutes to complete, and you will receive your results immediately.

Here are a few tips for taking the assessment:

Give yourself plenty of time. While it only takes thirty minutes, allow yourself enough time to fully think through each question to improve the accuracy of the results.

Be certain in your answers. The assessment asks you to evaluate certain statements on a scale from Not Satisfying to Most Deeply Satisfying. If you answer Most Deeply Satisfying too often, it can cloud the results.

Don't think too much. While it's important to consider each question, don't spend too much time looking for hidden meanings. Your gut response is probably the correct one.

Step Three: Explore the Results

Now that you've taken the MCODE assessment, it's time to find out what drives you.

Read the report. You will receive a report revealing your top three motivational themes. Your top three themes are what drive engagement and satisfaction in life and work. As mentioned above, these primary motivations interplay with one another, and it's likely you'll see traces of each of them in your achievement stories.

Read the sections describing your top three themes. The following sections in this book address each theme individually, sharing its unique characteristics, its potential shadow side, how to work with someone who is motivated in this way, and the kinds of roles in which a person motivated by the theme will thrive. As you read the section about each of your top themes, consider how that motivation may have influenced your decisions, behavior, and engagement over time.

There are no "good" themes or "bad" themes. Every form of motivation is a gift, and when activated can lead to brilliant work and deep satisfaction. Your themes simply describe where you get your motivational energy. You'll find professionals driven by every one of the twenty-seven themes at the very top of their industry, leading cultural change, and finding great success with their personal goals.

While you may initially wish to obtain your motivational energy elsewhere, remember that the world needs you to embrace the way you are wired. Receive what you're discovering about yourself, and put it into action. Your finest and most satisfying achievements will be accomplished when you work *with* your internal wiring—not *against* it.

Also, please note that not everything in the description of a particular theme might feel relevant to you. This is due to the reality, noted above, that motivational themes modify one another. So depending on your particular combination of top three themes, your practical experience of those motivations might differ slightly. However, it's likely that there will be much in the theme descriptions that fits you well.

Step Four: Discuss with a Peer

We all have blind spots. There are aspects of our behavior and personality that we can't see because they are simply habitual. This is why, in order to truly understand ourselves, we need the perspective of others. Therefore, we strongly recommend that you engage in this self-discovery process with at least one other person, so you can discuss the results of your assessment and its implications with a trusted peer, gain their perspective, and allow them to reflect back to you how they see your Motivation Code playing out in everyday life.

Here are a few questions you can discuss with a peer:

1. What surprised you about the results in the report? Is there anything about your Motivation Code you didn't expect to discover? Why?
2. How does uncovering your Motivation Code help you understand your past decisions, career moves, conflicts, and managerial style?

3. What didn't make sense? It's likely there are ways your Motivation Code doesn't perfectly align with what you anticipated. Sometimes this is because what you *wish* motivated you doesn't align with what *truly* drives you. Or it could be that the achievement stories you selected illustrated just one side of your motivation, but didn't tell the complete story.
4. What's next? Knowing what drives you matters very little if you don't put it into action. Now that you've discovered your Motivation Code, what are some steps you can take to implement your motivations into your work each day? Make a plan and hold each other accountable. (More about how to do this in chapter 9.)

A few things before we move forward. Each of the following chapters addresses a motivational family. You might be tempted to skip over a particular chapter if you don't believe it to be relevant, but I encourage you to dive in anyway. Understanding each of the motivational themes can help you better empathize with the needs and behaviors of your peers, family, and friends.

As you read on, consider situations in your life where you have interacted with someone who may have exhibited a particular motivational theme. Pay special attention to those moments when there was a misunderstanding or confusion, how it was handled, and how it might have been handled differently.

Also, I have tried to prune much of the data and science behind our research from the text, but if you'd like more detail, skip ahead to the appendices at the end of the book or visit motivationcode.com/science. There, you will find details about how the research was conducted, including information about the decades of achievement story analysis that led to the development of Motivation Code. You'll also find additional references and source material to help you dive deeper into motivational theory.

PART II
THE MOTIVATIONAL THEMES

Chapter Three

THE VISIONARY FAMILY

Common Characteristics

- Motivated to make an impact according to what is possible or ideal
- Fueled to turn ideas into reality, especially when they are the only one who thinks it's possible
- Able to spot the potential
- Future focused, sometimes at the expense of the present

THE MOTIVATIONAL THEMES IN THE VISIONARY FAMILY REVOLVE AROUND possibility. Those motivated in this way are driven to work *toward* something, even when others can't see or understand what they're so obsessed with. They often get bored when talking about logistics or processes, and instead want to focus on the big picture and the impact a project will have. They craft a vision that represents what could be, and then strive to bring that vision to concrete expression.

There are three key motivational themes that belong to the Visionary Family:

1. Achieve Potential
2. Make an Impact
3. Experience the Ideal

1: ACHIEVE POTENTIAL

Identifying and realizing potential is a constant focus of your activities.

When Sally started her new role as VP of talent development, she jumped in with both feet. If she was going to help improve her organization's performance, she thought, she needed a stronger team. In her first two years on the job, Sally selected a diverse group of skilled HR and training professionals. At the helm, Sally mentored and supported her team to foster their growth and challenge them to be effective leaders. Together, they created a pipeline of talent for the future and developed tools to attract new employees and measure progress and achievement. They also cultivated deep relationships with the leaders of each major division. As a result of her work, Sally and her team made a lasting, positive impact on the organization.

When asked what was most satisfying about this particular achievement, Sally said that she enjoyed creating a strategy for growing a business, implementing tactical plans, and measuring achievement. She especially loved to mentor young people and give them opportunities to grow and develop their talents while challenging them to be strong and confident. To Sally, developing close relationships with her team gave her joy. This was her Achieve Potential motivation at work.

Aiming for the Best

Like Sally, people driven by the desire to Achieve Potential feel a need to make things the best they can be and maximize their own platform for impact and expression. They are able to see beyond surface-level opportunities and identify and leverage connections that may not yet be obvious to others. Because of this, they are often a bit ahead of everyone else and can frustrate those who don't think the way they do.

Averse to Wasted Potential

Individuals with this motivational theme are driven to develop the potential they see, and aren't satisfied when they find that others are allowing value to be wasted. Perhaps surprisingly, they don't necessarily feel the need to be recognized for their work and are often perfectly fine with others getting the "glory" as long as the opportunity is leveraged and maximized. Their joy is in illuminating the possibility and seeing it put into play.

Many coaches in both athletics and business are driven by the Achieve Potential motivational theme. They find joy in helping others identify possibilities and accomplish their goals, and they're especially pleased when they unearth aptitudes or possibilities that others can't see in themselves. Many entrepreneurs have Achieve Potential among their top motivations. These individuals are able to spot opportunities in the marketplace that others may have missed and fill a need that's underserved.

The Shadow Side

There are some shadow-side attributes of the Achieve Potential motivational theme that can cause problems if not managed well:

THEY CAN HAVE UNREALISTIC EXPECTATIONS

Sometimes, those with an Achieve Potential theme can see all the ways something could be valuable or effective, but overlook obvious hurdles that might make their ideas unrealistic in the grand scheme. While their unbounded optimism and "get to it" attitude can be infectious in the right settings, they can also wear down a team of practical-minded professionals. Because of this, it's important to monitor their ideas to ensure they aren't seduced by sheer potential without considering the potential pitfalls.

THEY SEE LIFE AS OUT THERE INSTEAD OF RIGHT HERE

People motivated by the need to Achieve Potential often look far down the road, imagining possibilities and dreaming up scenarios rather than focusing on what's here, now, and urgent. As a result, they might overlook pressing problems and instead invest in projects that have a much longer payoff. This can benefit an organization over the long run, but not if immediate responsibilities are neglected. For that reason, these individuals often need help setting and maintaining priorities so they aren't lured away from the needs of the present.

THEY SPEND MORE TIME DREAMING THAN DOING

While those with an Achieve Potential motivational theme create grand plans for the future, playing with ideas and imagining what could be, they often struggle to make traction. Planning the practical next steps that will allow their plan to succeed sometimes makes them spin their wheels.

THEY PUT A POSITIVE SPIN ON EVERYTHING

While it sometimes pays to be optimistic in the face of adversity, those motivated by the need to Achieve Potential tend to put a positive, and at times unrealistic, spin on problems. They want so badly to see what something can become that they believe everything will work out in their favor if given enough time. However, when it's time to recognize failure for what it is and move on, those with this theme tend to struggle. Because of this, they can mislead team members and organizations who rely on their assessment of a project.

Working with an Achieve Potential Person

One of the challenges of working with a person with Achieve Potential as a top motivational theme is that while their ability to see what *could* be is one of their greatest assets, it's also what gets them into trouble. Therefore, they need help being realistic without having their enthusiasm squelched. They require the right level of support for their vision—without too much encouragement in the direction of risky ventures. The best way to do this is to ask a lot of practical questions to get them thinking about the specific steps they'd need to take to realize their vision. You could say, That's an interesting idea, and ask:

- Can you explain to me the steps you'll take to accomplish that?
- How will you know when the idea no longer has merit?
- How will you know when it's time to give up on the idea?

Those with a strong need to Achieve Potential are also wired for work that allows them to stretch their skills, maximize potential, and explore possibilities. Therefore, they tend to excel when given ownership of projects. It pays to spend time dreaming with them and allow their optimism to drive the conversation.

At the same time, because those with a strong Achieve Potential motivation see the possibilities in everything, they can sometimes become paralyzed. They require help narrowing down options so they aren't overwhelmed with what to do next. But long after others on the team have thrown in the towel, people with the need to Achieve Potential might want to persist. For this reason, it's important to keep an eye on areas where they may be disrupting the team dynamic.

When working with a person driven to Achieve Potential, be aware that not everything they suggest is a mandate for action; while they will likely share a lot of ideas for how things could be, that doesn't mean any of them will be executed. Rather, listen for actionable language, and ask about their specific expectations rather than inferring expectations from your conversations. For example, you could ask:

- Is there anything you'd like me to do about that project right now?
- To clarify, are we changing our client strategy?
- Is that the direction you'd like me to start working in? Or would you like me to wait until you've settled on the right approach?

Also, watch out for language that suggests the Achieve Potential–motivated person has a skewed view of reality, such as "this is the most important thing we've ever worked on" or "this is going to change the world." Clarify the difference between what's actually happening and what they believe *might* happen if only given enough time.

Where They Thrive

EARLY STAGES

A person with Achieve Potential as a top motivational theme will struggle in a role where their workload and strategies are directly dictated to them, or where information is withheld. For that reason, they need a lot of freedom and latitude in their work. They tend to thrive in the early stages of new ventures, especially those focused on launching a new product or industry or reimagining the state of the world. They also succeed in artistic and creative roles such as branding, design, and marketing, where the primary objective is to imagine a future state and figure out how to navigate toward it.

NEW PROJECTS

People with a need to Achieve Potential may tend to grow bored after a short season with long-arc projects. Even if they were previously enthusiastic, once a project is close to completion, they will lose interest and begin to shift their energy to newer, bigger, and better things. It's important to make sure that whatever work they do as a core part of their role includes new, big projects to envision and tackle.

VARIETY AND DIVERSITY

Those with Achieve Potential as a top motivational theme crave a variety of problems to solve and will quickly grow bored if tasked with tackling the same issue over and over, even if presented in slightly different contexts. Because of this, they don't do well in jobs with a fixed product where they must apply one solution from client to client. Instead, they prefer to imagine possible solutions that require them to think in new ways.

2: MAKE AN IMPACT

You seek to make an impact or personal mark upon the world around you.

From the moment Joseph was assigned to a project, his presence was felt. While many people would wait until they were acclimated to the team before speaking up, he certainly didn't feel the need to do so. From day one, he would try to change the team's mind-set about what they were doing, asking probing questions about why things were being done a certain way and suggesting actions he believed could make their processes more effective. Eventually, the project would usually go in a positive direction no one had envisioned before Joseph joined the team.

Like Joseph, people with Make an Impact as a top motivational theme are driven by a desire to see their unique, personal impact on others and the world around them. They want to step back at the end of their labor and see a real, concrete difference because of what they've done. It's important for them to know that things improved due to their personal efforts, so when that impact isn't plainly visible, they will be less motivated to engage in similar types of work again.

Able to Influence Anything

People with the need to Make an Impact have a strong desire to influence institutions, teams, processes, systems, and beliefs. It's important to them to have a lot of leeway to engage as they believe best and to shape things according to their intuition. People with this motivational theme include coaches, mentors, and leaders. They organize marches to raise awareness of issues in their community, volunteer at their child's school's PTO, and even run for local office.

Against the Status Quo

Those driven to Make an Impact are extremely intolerant of the status quo, especially when it's holding others back. They are often the first to step up and articulate how things could be different, then mobilize efforts to create that necessary change. They are also not afraid to take risks and introduce new ways of thinking into an organization, which can at times threaten the "old guard." For that reason, many people with this motivational theme are drawn to the arts, where challenging longtime conventions is not only normal but expected.

Eager to Leap First

Those fueled by the need to Make an Impact often jump into an uncomfortable role and take on challenging work, especially when they know the work has the potential to be noteworthy or could have a lasting impact on the future of the organization. When the potential is less clear, they might not be as committed.

The Shadow Side

While there are many positive attributes of someone driven to Make an Impact, there are also some potential watch points that they, their peers, and their manager should be mindful of:

THEY TEND TO MAKE CHANGES AND MEDDLE NEEDLESSLY

Because they are driven to make a significant impression on their organizations and those around them, people with Make an Impact as a top motivational theme tend to insert themselves where they may not be wanted or where someone else has authority. They can also reorganize and redefine problems just to make their mark on the world around them. For example, a sales associate may negotiate with clients without his supervisor's approval and accidentally promise more than he can deliver. Or a manager may adjust objectives every few weeks just to show he is contributing, and cause his confused team to underperform.

THEY HAVE DIFFICULTY SUBMITTING TO AUTHORITY

Those who want to Make an Impact need the freedom to pursue their ideas in a way they see fit. As a result, they often find it difficult to bend to the opinions of others and instead may work around or ignore them completely. They might also feign submission to authority but secretly work on projects behind the scenes.

THEY WITHDRAW WHEN THEIR IDEAS AREN'T ACCEPTED

If those with Make an Impact as a top motivation sense the group isn't going to comply with their vision, they will withdraw emotionally, mentally, or even physically and seek another place to exercise their talents. This can create tension within a team of many talented or Visionary-motivated people, all of whom are vying to make a great impact on the project. For example, one creative director would resist any idea that wasn't his own; if he couldn't put his unique stamp on it, then he would make a halfhearted effort toward it or act passive-aggressively toward the team. As a result, the entire group had to contort their ideas to make them seem like they were *his* in order to gain his support, which eventually led to needless tension and infighting.

THEY HAVE A SURPLUS OF IDEAS

People driven to Make an Impact can sometimes have *too* many ideas, which may lead to frustration and cause others to eventually ignore their challenges and pleas to change.

THEY ARE IMPATIENT AND WANT IMMEDIATE ACTION

Those who wish to Make an Impact can also be oblivious to timing and strategy, because they want to see the necessary changes occur here and now, not at some yet-to-be-determined moment. This can lead to tension with their manager and leadership when they feel their desired impact is not coming to fruition quickly enough.

Working with a Make an Impact Person

While those with Make an Impact as a top motivation can carry a big load and seem to push the work along through sheer will, they quickly lose interest if they can't see a direct connection between what they're doing and the impact they're making. Therefore, there are several tips to keep in mind when working with this type:

SHOW HOW THEY IMPACT YOU AND THE TEAM

People motivated to Make an Impact need to see that their ideas and behaviors are influencing others and that they are a valuable contributor to the team. You can express this by crediting them in a meeting ("If you look at the marketing budget spreadsheet, which Tom organized so well for us, you'll see that . . ."), by approaching them directly ("Katia,

I've been mulling over your suggestion for the proposal, and I really appreciate that you . . ."), or by copying them on an email to your manager and citing the impact they've made on the project. Of course, this doesn't mean you should celebrate every idea—or hang it on the refrigerator like a proud parent. However, it's important that Make an Impact–motivated people know you recognize the contribution they are making.

DISCUSS BARRIERS

Talking through strategy with those motivated to Make an Impact helps them better understand the constraints that might be limiting the impact they desire to have. Whether in a formal one-on-one check-in or over a casual lunch, you can ask them about where they perceive their impact is being stifled, where they wish they had more freedom to act, and barriers to their plans that can't be overcome. Do *not* "power up" and tell them to just deal with it. Instead, exhibit empathy and help them understand the bigger picture.

BE MINDFUL OF POTENTIAL CONTROL ISSUES

When left unchecked, a person with a strong Make an Impact motivation can prevent others from speaking up freely and can breed unnecessary friction within a team. When that happens, pull them aside and help them understand that impact can also look like helping those around them achieve their potential, not just having their own way every time. Keep your eyes on any areas where they may be exhibiting an unhealthy level of control, or when they seem to need to be in the driver's seat at all times.

BE DIRECT

Those who desire to Make an Impact often have a strong wish to be impacted. However, don't allow their strong will or vision intimidate you, or send the message that there's something wrong with their desire to be a change agent. Instead, speak clearly and firmly with them and help direct that effort into positive channels.

ASK FOR FEEDBACK

Those with this motivational theme tend to become overly involved in others' work in unhelpful and direction-altering ways, often when there isn't time or resources to change course. To combat this, solicit their feedback early in a project, when it's actually helpful and actionable, rather than waiting for them to get involved later on when it's more challenging to change direction. Also, do not immediately reject their ideas, but instead ask them to more fully explain their rationale and try to articulate their position back to them.

Where They Thrive

ROLES THAT HAVE DIRECT INFLUENCE ON RESULTS

People driven to Make an Impact want to be close to the action and know that the work they do is directly affecting the outcome of a project or group effort. They want to be able to point to the final product and say, "If not for me and my strengths, this wouldn't be possible." For this reason, these individuals are less gratified by behind-the-scenes, supportive, or administrative roles, or tasks that are repetitive and process oriented. Instead, they prefer roles where they can clearly see the impact of their actions on the bigger picture of the organization or its employees and clients.

THE GREAT UNKNOWN

Those with Make an Impact as a top motivation also perform well in environments requiring a lot of creative initiative, such as new organizations, the early stages of projects, or even moon-shot initiatives in which they must jump into the deep end and figure things out as they go. It's not because they are drawn to difficult work, but because these are the kinds of roles that contain opportunities for big, visible impact.

ROLES THAT GIVE THEM A WIDE BERTH

Because people with Make an Impact as a top motivation struggle to submit to authority when they feel their ideas aren't being taken seriously, having a manager who provides a good degree of freedom, within defined boundaries, is conducive to deeply satisfying work and productive influence.

3: EXPERIENCE THE IDEAL

You are motivated to give concrete expression to concepts, visions, or values that are important to you.

Nick always has a project in the works. Over the past several years, he has launched a number of companies, many of which have been highly successful and garnered massive media attention. He is constantly telling others about the latest product he's working on, and how excited he is to launch it into the world. He explains his vision in detail, how it's going to play out—even what his exit plan will be. Because of his contagious enthusiasm, Nick has attracted many successful partners, including celebrities, to help him turn his ideas into reality.

Biased to Journey over Destination

Those motivated to Experience the Ideal, like Nick, are passionate about turning things that are abstract, intangible, or ethereal into something concrete and valuable in the real world. This could mean transforming a far-off vision into a business or system, or pursuing justice for a particular cause. Many are entrepreneurs, intrepreneurs (people who innovate inside of larger organizations rather than starting their own company), business leaders, communicators, leaders of movements, or involved in some other vocation for a worthy cause. The pursuit of what could be, not the end result, is what's especially motivating.

Eager to Attain the Perfect Self

People with a strong drive to Experience the Ideal seek to be the most perfect version of themselves, so they tend to have high ideals, integrity, and very clear boundaries for what's acceptable and what's not.

Often Have Their Head in the Clouds

Those with Experience the Ideal as a top motivation are often highly creative and intuitive. They can see connections others can't yet and are prone to getting a few steps ahead of everyone else. They are also very conceptual, which means they tend to speak in abstractions rather than concrete and actionable ways. While this can make them seem like they have their head in the clouds or they are just dreamers, Experience the Ideal–motivated people are simply able to step back and see the full picture long before others. For this reason, they might need to frequently pause and explain their thoughts and behaviors so that everyone else can keep up.

The Shadow Side

Here are a few potential pitfalls that someone with Experience the Ideal as a top motivation is likely to encounter:

THEY GET FRUSTRATED WHEN THINGS AREN'T AS THEY "SHOULD" BE

Because those motivated to Experience the Ideal are focused on an imagined future and the way things would be if they were only set right, they can become frustrated when the reality doesn't align with their vision. So when an organization isn't living up to its mission in some way or a project requires compromise that will alter the intended outcome, these individuals might become so disappointed that they move their attention to another effort where they believe they can make headway toward their desired goals.

THEY ARE PERFECTIONISTS

Just as those driven to Experience the Ideal can become frustrated with reality, they can also be intolerant of any area where they perceive they themselves are falling short, or when their life doesn't reflect their ideal of how it should be. They may establish "rules" to help them pursue their values, but these can also make them inflexible in relationships requiring nuance or compromise. For example, if unexpected circumstances temporarily derail the pursuit of their vision, they can become frustrated in ways other-motivated people might not until they get back on track.

THEY STRUGGLE TO FACE REALITY

Those with Experience the Ideal as a top motivation are big-idea people who can see possibility everywhere, but this can prevent them from acknowledging when something simply isn't working, make it hard to be flexible and open-minded, and find them missing key problems. In some cases, this struggle to face reality might cause them to take wild risks that don't pay off, keep pouring money and energy into failing projects, or overestimate their team's and their own capabilities—in other words, they can miss the forest for the trees.

THEY WANT IT THEIR WAY OR NO WAY AT ALL

Individuals motivated to Experience the Ideal tend to refuse to compromise their vision in order to meld with the group consensus or anyone else's "less ideal" vision. Instead, they stand their ground.

Working with an Experience the Ideal Person

HELP THEM DISCERN WHETHER THEIR VISION IS REALISTIC

While you do want to encourage those with a strong desire to Experience the Ideal to think big and get out of their comfort zone, it's equally important that you help them realize what's practical given organizational resources and expectations. Have regular conversations with them about their ideas, and ask questions like:

- How realistic is this?
- How will you know when you have succeeded?
- How will you know if you need to change your strategy?

Don't force your perspective on them, but coach, ask questions, and guide them to come to reasonable conclusions on their own.

REFRAME THEIR DEFINITION OF "IDEAL"

How you define success often defines you, so it's important that those motivated to Experience the Ideal understand what success, not their idea of it, will actually look like in terms of organizational resources ("Although we only have the budget to complete eighty percent of your proposal, we consider this a success"), time frame ("Great idea, but this is a low priority since the deadline is Tuesday"), and their own capabilities ("I'm not sure you're quite ready to present to the entire organization, but let's work on those skills for next year"). This way, you are helping them stay rooted in what's really possible while encouraging them to aspire toward their vision.

CHALLENGE THE ROLES THEY PERCEIVE THEY ARE PLAYING

Those motivated to Experience the Ideal often see themselves as being on a kind of crusade—they are the only ones who can set right the great wrongs they see perpetrated around them. However, this self-perception can be skewed, and they might assume more gravitas than they actually wield. For example, they might say:

- "I am the only one who can . . ."
- "I need to put a stop to that right now."
- "I don't understand why they can't see the plain truth . . ."

If you notice someone using extreme language or taking on more than they are capable of, help them find alignment between their self-perception and reality. For example, if a person on your team is convinced they are the only one who can tackle an objective, ask if there is anyone else they can ask for help with it. You can also share real-life examples and stories of others to show what pursuing an ideal can look like when done in a healthy way—by enlisting others to help with a cause without infringing upon the work of those around them. Those motivated to Experience the Ideal tend to find stories very motivating, especially if they point to a higher order or moral takeaway.

DREAM WITH THEM

Even if your natural inclination is toward the pragmatic and concrete, spend some time dreaming with those driven to Experience the Ideal about all that's possible. They might share big ideas and possibilities with you as they are still working out how they're going to achieve them. Or they might have many ideas they hold internally but haven't shared. (Many Experience the Ideal–motivated people are introverts and hold their ideal in private, only sharing their dreams when you draw them out.) They might also have a lot of things they want to pursue, even if they recognize they only have time for a few. Therefore, it's important they see that you are their ally and are willing to get a little uncomfortable, even when thinking about what the future could hold. In turn, they will be more willing to trust you when you need to curtail their wild imaginations.

MATCH GOALS WITH ABILITIES

Often, people driven to Experience the Ideal are drawn to work that is slightly above their level of competence. For that reason, keep your eye on areas where they might be in over their head, or where they seem to be asking for more than you think is wise given their strengths and experience. Remember that even if they have the intrinsic motivation to knock it out of the park, without the necessary skills they are destined to underperform.

ESTABLISH BOUNDARIES

Because those with Experience the Ideal as a top motivation will likely have a lot of ideas, working with them can be exciting. However, you must also prepare yourself for the inevitable unrealistic requests that you and your team may be asked to take on. When this happens, be direct and establish boundaries to protect your personal life. (Unless you're working the overnight desk in a police department, you don't have to reply to emails at midnight!) Also, don't get pulled into their "crusades." It's likely that everything will seem to be of magnified importance to them, so don't get drawn into their sense of urgency until it's apparent they've made up their mind. Instead, patiently go about your work until they make a specific request.

Where They Thrive

"CHANGE THE WORLD" ROLES

Those motivated to Experience the Ideal want to know that they are pursuing something worthwhile, so they thrive in organizations with ambitious agendas driven by a noble cause. Whether it's curing cancer in a research lab, solving world hunger in an international think tank, or developing an app to facilitate signing up for health care, they come alive when they are using their talents to chase a vision.

JOBS THAT REQUIRE INNOVATION

People with Experience the Ideal as a top motivation are extremely gifted at not only envisioning but working toward possible futures. Unlike those driven by other themes in the Visionary Family, which focus primarily on the ideals themselves, Experience the Ideal–motivated people want to put their schemes into action and are unsatisfied until the real world matches what's in their head. Roles in which they constantly have to construct and create something—whether that's an app, an event, a proposal, a website, or a product—are well suited for these people.

TASKS THAT ALLOW CONTINUOUS PERSONAL IMPROVEMENT

Because individuals driven to Experience the Ideal want to develop their skills and ideas to match who they are with their vision of themselves, they crave roles with plenty of opportunities for upward momentum through promotions, title changes, and increased work. They also benefit from professional development in the form of in-house trainings, seminars, mentoring programs, and one-on-one check-ins. They prefer jobs that allow them to continuously pursue their ideal vision of life and work.

THE VISIONARY FAMILY: SUMMARY

If one of the themes that makes up your Motivation Code falls within the Visionary Family, there are a few practical things you can do to ensure you remain viable and productive over the long term:

Form Your Collective

Build relationships with people who can help you stay aware of areas where your optimism and desire for greater achievement may rise to unhealthy or unrealistic levels. Having a solid group of respected people around with whom you can share ideas, seek advice, and dream can make all the difference between a life spent creating a remarkable body of work and one of constant burnout. Find these people now and give them a window into your decision making.

Pause and Clarify

Because your vision can be clear in your own mind, remember that you will likely be several steps ahead of others. If you notice tension within the group, there's a good chance it's because you're making intuitive leaps that team members aren't following. Therefore, to keep your team in the loop, you may need to pause and explain your thoughts and actions often.

Take Time to Dream

So much of organizational life is about what's practical and imminent, which can squeeze the life out of those driven by motivations within the Visionary Family. Therefore, it's important that you schedule time into your daily life for thinking and dreaming. On your calendar, set aside an hour or two each week when you will write out ideas in a journal, take a long walk, and allow yourself to dwell in possibility for a while.

Mind Your Ideals

While it's wonderful to have a compass pointing to the future, it's necessary that you are mindful of how realistic your ideals are, especially given existing resource constraints and the goals of your team. You will be tempted to chase ideas that are simply out of range for you, or might find that you're taking on work that you cannot reasonably accomplish. But this is a recipe for burnout and frustration. Be mindful of areas in which your idealism might actually be stretching you too thin.

Be a Supporter, Not a Detractor

Finally, send clear signals to your team that you are on the same page and will use your talents to help accomplish the overall mission, even if you believe more is possible. There are a few ways you can do this:

- Hold back from speaking up first in a meeting
- Say a simple "thank you"
- Compliment someone else's idea
- Give credit where credit is due
- Don't chirp about wasted potential or small goals
- Do your job, but keep your eye on the horizon

Understanding your natural motivation will help funnel that Visionary energy in more helpful and productive ways.

Those whose Motivation Code is made up of themes under the Visionary Family propel us into the future. It is their desire to push toward the ideal and realize their dreams that pulls the rest of us along, even if unwittingly at times. In an organization, they are often the ones who ask the inconvenient questions and challenge their teams to continue climbing that mountain when things get difficult.

Chapter Four

THE ACHIEVER FAMILY

Common Characteristics

- Driven to persevere through challenges
- Motivated to overcome obstacles and oppose an "enemy"
- Want to complete tasks, even at the expense of eating and sleeping
- Engaged when making progress

HAVE YOU EVER MADE A FIFTEEN-PAGE BUDGETING SPREADSHEET TO KEEP track of your spending and updated it every single day? Have you been the only one to volunteer to lead a project that was almost certain to fail? Do you find yourself rooting for the underdog, whether you're watching a basketball game or helping a colleague prep for a promotion? If you answer yes to any or all of these questions, it's very likely that at least one of the motivational themes that make up your Motivation Code falls within the Achiever Family.

Those driven by the Achiever themes are rarely satisfied with half measures. They are the ones barking at the group to continue moving forward, persist when times get tough, and keep their eyes on the prize. For them, satisfaction is not necessarily derived from recognition or being the person in charge—in fact, many of them are behind-the-scenes people—but is about their innate desire to prove to themselves and others that they can do something many think is impossible. They will not let themselves or others down.

There are four motivational themes within the Achiever Family:

1. Meet the Challenge
2. Overcome
3. Bring to Completion
4. Advance

4: MEET THE CHALLENGE

Your sense of achievement comes from looking back over a challenge you have met or a test you have passed.

I am normally a productive and focused person. However, because my Motivation Code includes Meet the Challenge as my second strongest motivation, this means that I occasionally drift into less industrious, but nonetheless very motivating, activities.

Enter the video game *Fortnite*. In my entire adult life, I have probably played a grand total of ten hours of video games. But a few years ago, my teenage son introduced me to a new video game he discovered. For the uninitiated, let me set the stage: In *Fortnite*, you are dropped onto an island with ninety-nine other players. You choose where you land, collect weapons in order to survive, and eliminate other players. The objective of the game is to be the last survivor.

In my first time playing, I landed on the island and was eliminated within seconds. "This is stupid," I said. Then I started over. The second time I played, I lasted a few minutes. The third time, a few minutes more. By the end of the night, I'd played a dozen games and managed to be among fifty top players. A few months later, I cracked the top ten. Finally, one night I achieved my first victory. I let out a whoop and explained to my wife what had happened. "Great job beating that seven-year-old, honey!" she replied.

Here's why playing *Fortnite* is dangerous to a Meet the Challenge–motivated person:

- The rules are simple—there is just one winner
- Each game lasts only about fifteen to twenty minutes
- Winning requires both skill and luck; you can improve, but your success also depends on the choices other players make
- The results are easily measurable—either you won, or you didn't

When my work—such as book writing or long-arc client tasks—doesn't have sufficient and frequent challenges to conquer, I will go elsewhere.

Relentlessly Persistent

Those who are driven to Meet the Challenge are deeply motivated by difficult tests of skill, understanding, or endurance. For them, it's not about whether they win or are seen as excellent, but that they manage to tackle the obstacle. Adopting a don't-tell-me-what-I-can't-do mindset, they will stretch themselves, even to the point of burnout, in the face of difficult odds. As a result, they tend to be the first to volunteer for seemingly impossible tasks, and their achievement stories often involve adversity or time-consuming projects.

In an interview, actor Will Smith said, "The only thing that I see that is distinctly different about me is I'm not afraid to die on a treadmill. I will not be out-worked, period. You might have more talent than me, you might be smarter than me, you might be sexier than me, you might be all of those things—you got it on me in nine categories. But if we get on the treadmill together, there's two things: You're getting off first, or I'm going to die. It's really that simple, right?" This is a classic Meet the Challenge mind-set—when confronted with a challenger, Smith is willing to do whatever is necessary to prove he's up to the task.

> **You Might Be Motivated to Meet the Challenge If You . . .**
>
> - Go door-to-door to hundreds of homes to get enough signatures for a petition.
> - Climb a mountain . . . just because it's there.
> - Accept a work task that no one else wants, then complete it in record time.
> - Finish an ultramarathon. Or any marathon.
> - Can't walk away from a carnival game until you win.

Competitive

People who have Meet the Challenge as a top motivation seek challenges everywhere, even in places where they don't exist. For instance, they may propose more ideas than anyone else in a meeting or make more sales calls before noon than their peers make in a day. As a result, they can create an environment of competition where one isn't warranted.

Fueled by High Stakes

These individuals tend to also work well under pressure and are especially good at performing within tight deadlines, which tend to impose a do-or-die layer of challenge onto the work.

Able to Keep Their Eyes on the Prize

People with Meet the Challenge as a top motivation are good at focusing on just the essential elements necessary to accomplish something—they don't get lost in details or distracted by sidetrack issues. Instead, they keep their eyes on the prize and tunnel their way toward it with precision and determination. For example, these individuals might stick with a marketing strategy longer than others because they know they can find a way to make it work, or continue taking the most difficult class offered by their university in spite of the struggle because they want to prove they can do it.

Willing to Pick Up the Slack

Finally, these individuals tend to be the team member who will rise to the occasion and get results. Although they might fly under the radar for a while, they will suddenly appear just when needed most and pick up the mantle of responsibility. They are often only fueled to work when it's "game time," or when the work really matters, such as near the finish line of a project, when an unexpected issue comes up, or when someone on the team drops the ball.

The Shadow Side

Those motivated to Meet the Challenge are driven to achieve results, but that desire can also have unintended consequences. Here are a few of those pitfalls:

THEY SEE ROUTINE TASKS AS CHORES

Sometimes, people with Meet the Challenge as a top motivation may struggle to do any work that doesn't feel like a challenge. That's why routine maintenance, repetitive tasks, and other types of administrative work like filing, creating spreadsheets, and making phone calls might be unbearable to this individual. They might find (or create) problems that don't really need to be solved, or turn the routine work into a competitive game just to have a challenge to overcome. Eventually, they might seek challenge in places where it's not helpful to their team or the organization.

THEY ARE PRONE TO PROCRASTINATION

Because those driven to Meet the Challenge need an obstacle to feel fully engaged, they might fabricate one by putting off important work until there's pressure to get it done. For example, a leader of a creative team once said that he could have weeks to come up with a strategy for his next client pitch, but would put off brainstorming until a day or two before the meeting because he felt he performed best when under pressure. While he may have performed just fine in this manner, his team didn't always have the information or time they needed to do their best work and often had to scramble at the last minute to pull things together. If the leader had understood why he required pressure to feel motivated and adapted his behavior accordingly, he and his team may have had more successful pitches.

THEY ARE WILLING TO ASSUME UNNECESSARY RISK

Because they crave the adrenaline rush, those who need to Meet the Challenge might assume more risk than is wise or make needlessly reckless decisions. They might even create a crisis just to have something to fix—for example, taking a big gamble with a client pitch at the last minute because they want to see if they can pull it off, or hiking solo on a dangerous, mountainous stretch of trail because they don't want to wait until they have someone with them.

THEY CAN HAVE EXCESSIVE TUNNEL VISION

They might block out anything not associated with the challenge they're currently pursuing. They only pay attention to those ideas and people that are useful at the moment for meeting that challenge, which can leave team members feeling ignored or undervalued. When Meet the Challenge–driven individuals are obsessed with proving they can do something, everything else in their world often gets filtered through that challenge. They might be neglectful of people around them who depend on them, or they might ignore the emotional needs of their team if addressing them means taking their eye off the challenge.

THEY ARE PREDISPOSED TO UNHEALTHY LEVELS OF STRESS

Because of their need to perform under pressure, those motivated to Meet the Challenge tend to have very high levels of stress, which can cause negative health effects and affect their relationships with coworkers, family, and friends. They struggle with relaxing until they've met their goal, so they might not get the proper amount of sleep or recreation, might miss a meal or two without even realizing it, and will instead spend much of their waking time obsessing over how to achieve their objectives.

Working with a Meet the Challenge Person

CHECK TO SEE IF THEY ARE PUSHING THEMSELVES
OR OTHERS TOO HARD

If you begin to notice signs of excessive stress in a Meet the Challenge–motivated person, probe to see if you can discover the source. Even when it seems like everything is just fine, talk to them regularly about their level of stress to ensure they don't succumb to unrealistic expectations or push their team too hard. You might be uniquely positioned to help them identify those areas where they might be overextending.

At the same time, don't get drawn into their competitive energy. There's nothing wrong with spurring one another to do better work, but be mindful of the unhealthy competitive dynamics that can sometimes arise when these individuals collaborate with others. Do your best to mind your own reasonable timelines, and don't allow them to artificially rush your work because of their need for a challenge.

OPEN THEIR EYES TO THE BIG PICTURE

Remember that those who strive to Meet the Challenge often have tunnel vision and can ignore anything that doesn't help them achieve their objective. Therefore, use your time together to help them gain a more expansive view of what's going on in their work. Remind them that they don't want to sacrifice their long-term goals in their pursuit of a short-term challenge. Ask questions that allow them to reframe their priorities in light of the future, not just the task in front of them.

EXPLORE THE DIFFERENCE BETWEEN "CAN DO" SKILLS AND "LOVE TO DO" TALENTS

Because those driven to Meet the Challenge are so focused on getting results, they often engage in work they'd prefer not to do, but that gives them a sense of having ticked off a task on a to-do list, such as answering emails and organizing the mail room. For this reason, it's important to help them explore how much of the work they are currently doing is for true enjoyment versus their need to accomplish. Guide them in identifying areas where they might be able to incorporate "love to do" talents in their work.

BE DIRECT AND GET TO THE BOTTOM LINE

When working with those who have Meet the Challenge as a top motivation, it's important to recognize that their timelines might not match yours, and that their expectations of themselves might translate into unhealthy expectations of you as well. These individuals also tend to be intolerant of ambiguous language and anything that doesn't point toward results. For that reason, keep the lines of communication direct and clear—don't beat around the bush. Make sure you are regularly touching base with them about objectives, time frames, and expectations so you're both on the same page, and get to the point quickly when discussing a problem. Be up front with them about your available resources, your energy level, and the amount of time you're spending on projects, and have data to back up your assertions. You could say, for example, "I'm excited about this new project, but I'm concerned that we can't do it well while finishing our other work. Can we begin next week?"

CREATE TARGETED ACTION PLANS

If you want to get the attention of someone motivated to Meet the Challenge, make sure you are using concrete methods for tracking progress. Break larger projects down into smaller objectives with frequent checkpoints, regular opportunities for feedback, and challenging, but achievable, goals. Objectives that can't be easily measured don't usually work with them. Don't allow them to artificially escalate expectations, but keep them inside the bounds of what's reasonable.

STRETCH THEM OUT OF THEIR COMFORT ZONE

Meet the Challenge–motivated people come alive when they're given the chance to step up and deliver results at key moments. So don't be afraid to issue challenges—it's what drives them—as long as you are mindful of their tendency to overwork and live with stress. However, as we mention above, make sure you do have regular conversations with them about how they are balancing all areas of their life so that your challenge doesn't become an excuse to neglect their relationships or personal priorities.

Where They Thrive

PROJECTS WHERE THEY CAN CONCRETELY MEASURE RESULTS

Meet the Challenge–driven people want to know whether they've "won." They perform best in jobs that require short-to-medium bursts of extreme effort that end in either success or failure. In other words, there needs to be a grading scale by which they can measure their efforts, such as an annual sales target, getting a book on the bestseller list, acquiring a client, or securing a difficult contract. If for too long these individuals are in a more process-oriented role with an ambiguous definition of success and no clear outcome, they will grow disenchanted. Long, slogging marathon jobs are not for them.

WHERE THERE'S A CLEAR SCOREBOARD

Clear and public goals can raise everyone's game, but they're especially motivating to those fueled to Meet the Challenge. That's why they are well suited for sales, business development, and other roles that allow for a lot of short-term wins and have a public scoreboard that let them easily challenge themselves. However, it's important that they not lose themselves in the challenge and forget about the ultimate objective, which is to contribute to the success of the organization.

"I DON'T KNOW IF THIS IS POSSIBLE, BUT . . ." ROLES

These words are magic to the Meet the Challenge person. If you want them on board with an idea, just tell them they can't do it and they will have it done before lunchtime. They love to jump in with both feet and figure it out as they go. However, this can sometimes mean that they get in over their head, so helping them shape and define the workflow can be critical to their long-term health and success.

5: OVERCOME

Your motivation focuses on overcoming and triumphing over difficulties, disadvantages, or opposition.

During a basketball game in my sophomore year of high school, I felt a slight twinge in my back. Initially, I thought I could stretch to get rid of it, but it wouldn't go away. Later that night, I awoke with a shooting pain up and down my back, unable to move my legs. I rolled over and crawled to the hallway, where I screamed for my parents. I was quickly shuttled to the local hospital.

Upon doing a scan, the doctors discovered a mass in my abdomen: a muscle was swollen with a rare and dangerous infection and was now pressing tightly against the main nerve running down my back and legs. There was a lot of doubt about whether I would survive. The infection was so serious, in fact, that one of the doctors told my parents, "*If* I can save him . . ."—words you never want to hear. Thankfully, I was given an intense round of antibiotics and within a few weeks the infection was gone. But I'd arrived at the hospital as a six-foot-three, 185-pound athlete—I was now a 131-pound skeleton. Additionally, I'd lost nearly all the muscle in my lower body, so I couldn't move my legs, much less play basketball.

Back then, basketball was my true love. The thought of having to leave the sport was too much for me, so I resolved that I would prove them wrong, whatever it took. Over the next six months, I engaged in a physical therapy regimen so grueling that I often had to be treated on my own, because I would let out screams of pain as I attempted to walk. But after many months of ceaseless effort, I learned to walk again, built muscle, and regained my strength. That fall, I made the varsity team. And the following season, I averaged twenty points and ten rebounds per game and was voted district player of the year by area coaches.

I don't tell this story to relive the glory days—believe me, those years were anything but glorious. Rather, I share this to demonstrate how the drive to Overcome can lead people to surmount great odds in order to prove the naysayers wrong.

Journey over Destination

Those motivated to Overcome are driven to beat difficulties, disadvantages, and opposition. However, they derive their energy not from the completion of the task, but from the struggle against an "enemy." They sometimes see themselves as the underdog, needing to face up to a larger, more accomplished adversary. When sharing their story, they focus on the barriers that had to be crossed—in other words, what they were *against* more than what they were *for*. More than the end result, it's the process of conquering that excites them.

Unable to Quit

Overcome-motivated people tend to be very determined and can persevere in the face of difficulty long after others have given up. Because they derive their motivational energy from exerting sustained, all-out effort, they may stick with a project or problem long after others have given up, even when it seems the problem is impossible to solve. In fact, they may not be able or willing to concede defeat even when it's staring them in the face because they cannot comprehend a situation in which they don't overcome the obstacle. This makes them highly skilled at troubleshooting; you want to assign a person driven to Overcome your most difficult and unsolvable issue. This also makes them very competitive, although their competitive streak is often focused on overcoming the odds rather than simply winning.

Not Easily Intimidated

Those driven to Overcome are your "get it done" people. In fact, they may gain energy as things grow more difficult. They are not passive but willing to confront perceived evil head on. They do not shrink in the face of intimidation tactics, but instead will stand headstrong against them. They step into areas where there is perceived injustice, racism, or other discrimination when others stand passively by. They gain energy from fighting these battles.

Perceptive of Obstacles

These individuals are also skilled at identifying the key obstacles that stand in the way of their success and what it will take to surmount them. Because they are highly attuned to common problems, they can often spot patterns others overlook, such as potential marketplace competitors or probable flaws in research. They figure out what's getting in the way so they can defeat it.

The Shadow Side

For all of the wonderful, contributive qualities of a person with Overcome as a top motivation, there are also some negative attributes to be mindful of:

THEY CAN BE A SOURCE OF UNDUE STRESS TO THOSE AROUND THEM

Those motivated to Overcome are able to deal with high levels of stress. In fact, they often seek out stress because they derive energy from overcoming the very obstacles that create it. However, this can make them unaware of how their pursuit of stress can create unnecessary pressure on those who depend on them. If they lead a team, their pursuit of bigger and more challenging obstacles might create an atmosphere of perpetual anxiety for those who aren't necessarily wired to gain energy from high levels of stress.

THEY ARE TEMPTED TO CREATE OR INFLATE PROBLEMS

Just to have something to overcome, people with this motivation may create issues where none exist. Or they might identify "enemies" working against them just so they are operating from a posture of "overcomer." For this reason, those driven in this way tend to exaggerate the odds to create the illusion they are doing what seems impossible. They also might inflate the story to make an accomplishment sound much more impressive than it actually was.

> **Common Enemies of the Overcomer**
> - The biggest player ("giant") in their industry
> - Difficult coworkers who don't seem to "get it"
> - Seemingly pointless regulation or organizational bureaucracy
> - The other political party or proponent of an ideology they abhor

THEY CAN BE INAPPROPRIATELY COMBATIVE

People with the need to Overcome as a top motivation are prone to confront rather than compromise. They might blame others when they fail, or throw teammates under the bus when things don't go as planned. For example, one designer at a creative agency never seemed to like any ideas offered up by her peers. She would quickly point out the flaws in an idea as soon as it was suggested, without giving others time to consider it. Eventually, this caused everyone to hesitate before sharing a spark of insight. The designer's need to find and overcome obstacles was squelching the team's ability to have an open dialogue about possibilities.

THEY FIND IT HARD TO RELAX OR BE AT PEACE

Those who are Overcome-motivated are often on edge, looking for their next battle. They can't rest until they feel like they've won, but when they do, they immediately begin to seek a new boulder to push against. They move from obstacle to obstacle, struggling to celebrate success because they are always seeking the "next thing."

Working with an Overcome Person

BE PREPARED FOR CONFLICT

An individual motivated to Overcome may make comments like:

- "The problem with your idea is . . ."
- "Don't tell me what I can't do . . ."
- "No one will give me what I need to do my work . . ."

Recognize that their posture is to confront first and ask questions later, so don't take it personally—they are prone to seeing battle lines everywhere. Instead, help them recognize that you are on their side and aligned on desired outcomes, even if your ideas for how to achieve them are in conflict with theirs. Try to help them realize when they are turning molehills into mountains, and talk to them about their perception to unearth exactly what is driving their need for conflict. However, make certain you are managing the conflict in a healthy way so it doesn't overshadow your team's efforts. Define the disagreement in concrete terms, so as to prevent the Overcome-motivated individual from making it about some ideal or distant "enemy." Talk about specific differences of opinion but also areas of common ground so they don't overinflate the level of conflict. Finally, make sure the conflict is about ideas and not the personalities involved.

Also, don't take their combative nature personally—they probably like you (they do!). Recognize that their brashness and potentially offensive comments are not aimed at you, but are rather targeted at taking down some ideological enemy they see lurking. Getting defensive will only escalate the battle. Instead, say something like "I understand that you don't like my idea. Can we discuss any parts of it you do agree with, then discuss where we diverge?"

WATCH OUT FOR YOUR OWN STRESS

It's likely that the person driven to Overcome will bring high levels of stress into your relationship. Monitor this, and make certain you aren't allowing their drive to overshadow your conversations. Be aware of areas where they are creating problems that don't exist, or where their overly confrontational mind-set could be putting you on the defensive. Also, be mindful that you might be absorbing some of their stress and allowing it to affect your own work performance. The person motivated to Overcome might not recognize that you are wired differently and don't feel the same drive to surmount obstacles that they do. Don't allow yourself to be pulled into their personal battles, but maintain your objectivity and ability to guide them from a safe perch.

BE DIRECT WITH THEM

Overcome-motivated people will value and respect you more if you are honest with them and challenge them when it's appropriate to do so. Don't "power up" or create another obstacle for them to counter, but establish clear boundaries and share openly when you believe they are veering off course. Also, be mindful of how they tend to pull others into working more than necessary, to create excessively short timelines, or to tackle ridiculously ambitious projects. Talk with them about reasonable timelines and expectations while simultaneously reassuring them that you see their ambition and want to help them pursue their work in a way that gratifies them.

HELP THEM IDENTIFY THE COMMON GOOD

At times, the Overcomer will adopt a "me against the world" attitude, which positions them as the lone wolf trying to pursue justice. In the same way, they tend to see themselves as the underdog, which can lead to a sense of isolation. One way you can prevent them from slipping too deeply into this mind-set is by helping them understand how the battles they are fighting fit into the overall common good, and how their contributions are part of a larger team effort.

FACILITATE THE OVERCOMING OF SELF

The person driven to Overcome achieves maturity when they are able to firmly hold the reins of self-possession, meaning they can channel their need to overcome energy toward themselves rather than outside obstacles. For that reason, help them identify areas where their need to Overcome is working against their overall ability to function in a healthy way, both personally and professionally. Are they just looking for enemies to fight, or are they battling against a real obstacle? Coach them to channel that motivational energy in a more productive direction. The objective is to help them achieve a measure of peace even in the midst of their struggles to Overcome.

Where They Thrive

DIFFICULT CHALLENGES WITH A LONG TIMELINE

Those motivated to Overcome are more marathon runners than sprinters. The struggle itself is what motivates them, not the outcome. Building a company, working toward changing a government policy, or serving in leadership at a nonprofit seeking to right a social wrong are examples of roles where they might thrive. Whatever job they do, they need to ensure that they have a great cause to work toward and clear obstacles to surmount along the way.

ROLES WITH A CLEAR "ENEMY"

Because they tend to adopt a posture of being *against* rather than *for* and do their best work when they believe they alone are capable of righting a great wrong, it helps them to have a clear enemy to act in opposition to: a competitive company they believe isn't acting in the best interests of the customer, or a rival political figure they believe is misleading constituents.

BEING THE POINT PERSON

Those with Overcome as a top motivation want to dive into those thorny issues that no one else wants to tackle and bring clarity to long-standing problems, like fixing a corporate culture or restructuring the organization. While they might be a little abrasive from time to time, or lack tact, they will absolutely get the job done and it will be very clear where they stand at all times.

6: BRING TO COMPLETION

Your motivation is satisfied when you can look at a finished product or final result and know your work is done and you have met the objective you set out to accomplish.

When Elizabeth entered the field of business engineering, she immediately knew she'd found her professional home. Her job was all about staying organized, creating lists, and completing tasks. It also allowed her to drive big projects forward and break down goals into smaller, manageable wins. "I love lists and I couldn't work without them," she says. "What keeps me focused in my job is knowing that I only have an hour . . . so I need to get some writing done now!"

Elizabeth's Motivation Code has Bring to Completion as a top theme—and it's all about getting things done.

Inclined to Arrive at the End Result

People driven to Bring to Completion derive their primary motivational energy from pushing projects across the finish line. They are satisfied when they can look at the final product and know the work is done and the objective has been met. For this reason, it's important to them to recognize when something is complete, so they gravitate toward work that has a clear end point, like client projects and one-solution problems, rather than work that is iterative over months or years, like dealing with government regulations or engaging in long-term training or human resources work.

Process Oriented

Those driven to Bring to Completion tend to have a very clear understanding of what success will look like at the very beginning, so they sequence their efforts to arrive at the finish line in the most direct manner possible. Because they generally don't derive energy from the process as much as from the completion of the work, they are very efficient and process oriented. To them, a well-run system means more frequent trips across the finish line. Perhaps that's why they love lists—every item checked off is one step closer to accomplishment.

Able to Get Caught Up in Momentum

Those motivated to Bring to Completion can get caught up in the momentum of the work and have difficulty stopping until they're finished. They might stay up for hours into the night or work nonstop for weeks on end until they cross the finish line. As a result, they can also push those around them to work a little faster or harder, especially when they realize completion is within range. While this can create a lot of short-term wins for the team, it can also create a pressure-cooker environment over time.

Top Producers

People with Bring to Completion as a key motivation get a lot of things done and are often the top producers in the organization, attracting admiration for their ability to achieve results consistently over a long period of time. They don't spend hours thinking about the work, but instead dive in and push things forward.

The Shadow Side

Even as they create tremendous value by driving projects forward, there are a few shadow-side characteristics those motivated to Bring to Completion must be mindful of:

THEY CAN MISS THE FOREST FOR THE TREES

Because they are so focused on getting things done, they can fail to see opportunities to create more value since their primary concern is pushing the project across the finish line as efficiently as possible. They are often so obsessed with the work right in front of them, and what it will take to move that work forward, that they can't think long term or consider alternative possibilities.

THEY'RE UNABLE TO RELAX UNTIL THINGS ARE FINISHED

It can be difficult for those motivated to Bring to Completion to feel any sense of rest or peace when they know there's work to be done, or when something is so close to being done they know it will only take a bit of concentrated effort to finish it. At that point, anything other than working on that objective can feel like wasted time. Expecting others to follow their drive to complete things, even when it means compromising rest, can create an aura of restlessness on their team.

For example, one manager who oversaw the operations of a marketing team was unable to modify her expectations, even when someone on her team got sick. Although the group was shorthanded, the manager refused to slow down and allow the team to operate at a more reasonable pace, which led to seasons of burnout and disengagement.

THEY ARE PRONE TO MAKING MISTAKES

Because these individuals tend to move quickly through projects in order to complete them, they might miss details that are peripheral but important. They will almost always hit their target, but they might do so with minimum effort and low quality. This pattern is certainly something to keep an eye on, because while their efficiency is enviable, those motivated to Bring to Completion might create more to do for those around them if their own work isn't up to team standards. They will be thorough, as long as being thorough is on their list of things to do!

THEY ARE EASILY ANNOYED WHEN PLANS CHANGE

Those driven to Bring to Completion often have little tolerance for anything that prevents them from making progress. As a result, they tend to find meetings and inefficient systems useless—simply obstacles that stand in their way—and might even circumvent them altogether. They might also get short with anyone who disrupts their day or requires them to change plans. Anything that gets in the way of their ability to check a few items off their list will draw their ire.

Working with a Bring to Completion Person

A Bring to Completion–motivated individual's ability to "get it done" can be immensely valuable to a team, and indispensable at certain phases of a project, such as later stages when they are needed to take charge and push things forward. Encourage this instinct while also gently helping them see the wisdom in taking occasional pauses to seek the bigger strategic picture and align their efforts with the rest of the team.

HELP THEM EXPAND THEIR VISION OF WHAT'S POSSIBLE

Because it can be difficult to measure goals that take a long time to accomplish, those with Bring to Completion as a top motivation can sometimes become very focused on projects with shorter deadlines. Therefore, keep your eye on areas where they may be compromising long-term value to achieve short-term objectives. Question them about their decision making. Don't tell them what to do, but help them expand their perspective. Ask them about their future plans, their objectives for the next year, and other topics that require them to focus on the horizon, not the next few yards ahead of them. Then, ask how their present activity is going to help them achieve those goals.

To Guide a Bring to Completion Person Out of Tunnel Vision, Ask:

- What are your goals for the next year?
- Do you have any personal development objectives?
- What was the best book you've read in the last year, and how did it affect you?
- If you could snap your fingers and make it happen, what changes would you like to see over the coming quarter?

BE VERY PRACTICAL

Those driven to Bring to Completion have a low tolerance for conceptual conversations and are much more comfortable talking about tactics and strategy. Therefore, help them break down big goals into small, concrete steps so they are more likely to stay engaged as the project moves forward. Establish some clear milestones they can celebrate as they go. Their "wins" should be measured in days or weeks, not months or quarters.

ENCOURAGE THEM TO ASK FOR HELP

One of the qualities of the person motivated by Bring to Completion is that they will do whatever it takes to get a project done, even if they are not the right person to tackle a task. As a result, they tend to burn out more quickly than those around them. Help them differentiate between the work they should focus on and the work they should leave to others.

EXPLORE THEIR NEED FOR EMOTIONAL AND SPIRITUAL DEVELOPMENT

Because personal development, self-care, relationships, and community are aspects of human life more difficult to measure, those driven to Bring to Completion might subconsciously avoid cultivating these areas. Therefore, it's important to initiate discussions with them about non-work-related goals they might be neglecting in their perpetual race to the finish. Discuss with them ways in which they can incorporate these goals into their daily and weekly rhythms.

Five Non-Work Things for a Bring to Completion Person to Do

- Read five books in the next six months just for pleasure.
- Set a health goal (lose five pounds, run three miles a day) for the next quarter.
- Go to lunch once a week with a teammate and discuss non-work topics.
- Commit to a standard bedtime for the next month, and don't violate it even when trying to crank out a few last-minute emails.
- Take a walk during lunch break and listen to calming music.

Where They Thrive

PROJECT MANAGEMENT

Because individuals motivated to Bring to Completion need to keep pushing things forward, they can be valuable in roles requiring them to corral others' efforts. However, they need people around them who can help them see the big picture. In their efforts to push forward, they are prone to tunnel vision.

ROLES WITH SHORT TIMELINES

Their primary satisfaction comes from completing projects, so it's important they have clear and quick finish lines. If they are required to work on projects with very long deadlines and few checkpoints in the middle and that aren't easily measurable, they might lose interest. However, when there is a clear objective and time frame, and a critical path for accomplishment, they will be the driving force that propels the work forward.

ROLES WHERE THEY ARE PARTNERED WITH VISIONARIES

Those with Bring to Completion as a top motivation are skilled at bringing others' visions to life because they see how to execute plans and take them across the finish line—what Visionary-minded people often struggle with. As such, Bring to Completion–motivated people are especially productive when they are partnered with someone who can intuit where to go and imagine that better future.

7: ADVANCE

You love the experience of making progress as you accomplish a series of goals.

Referred to by his contemporaries as the "Prophet of Progress," Charles Kettering was an American inventor and engineer responsible for many functions still in use in modern automobiles, including the electrical starting motor. He equated technological advancement with human progress. Ever future focused, he once quipped, "I object to people running down the future. I am going to live all the rest of my life there." He believed that continual change is the only way to build a better, more promising world. "You will never stub your toe standing still," he said. "The faster you go, the more chance there is of stubbing your toe, but the more chance you have of getting somewhere."

Kettering is a great example of a person motivated to Advance.

All about the Process

People with Advance as part of their Motivation Code love the experience of making progress, and as long as they are making progress, the promise of completion keeps them engaged in the work. When things stall, or when the Advance-driven individual begins to sense momentum waning, they tend to lose interest. Therefore, having concrete, visible hurdles, however small, like project deadlines or well-defined problems, can help provide the motivation they need to keep going.

In a similar vein, those motivated to Advance are driven to continuous self-improvement. They often crave a sense of personal progress to stay engaged and energized. They are very likely to have a personal development plan that they follow daily for their fitness, education, and even finances.

Problem-Solving Machines

Advance-motivated people love to work on problems, and especially a sequence of problems to be solved over time—they are much less interested in optimizing or maintaining a system. For this reason, they tend to be quick to identify needs and tackle them before anyone else even knows the needs are there, as their constant desire to stay in motion makes them alert to opportunities to gain ground. When others don't immediately offer to help, they will tackle the problems themselves and catch their peers up once the issues are resolved.

Quick to Act

Those motivated to Advance are highly capable of executing their intuitions and ideas to accomplish their goals. They are not dreamers. On the other hand, they are very practical and quickly bring their ideas to real life. They want to be efficient, so they don't spend a lot of time ruminating on possible options or wavering over which path to take. Instead, they choose a course of action, act, learn, redirect, and make progress toward their central goal.

Resourceful

Those with Advance as a top motivation are also very resourceful. They don't wait for others to show them exactly how to get things done, but rather are able to identify what they'll need, organize around it, and figure out ways to succeed with whatever they have in front of them. To them, lack of time and resources is not an excuse for lack of progress.

The Shadow Side

As with the other motivations, the best traits of the Advance-motivated person can also at times be what holds them back. The need to make forward progress can actually blind them to the opportunities here and now. Here's how:

THEY HAVE DIFFICULTY ENJOYING THE PRESENT

Because those driven to Advance are perpetually thinking about the next step, conversation, or problem they need to tackle, they can struggle to remain present. They are often here and somewhere else at the same time mentally. This can be frustrating for those who need their full attention.

THEY ARE UNABLE TO BE CONTENT

Those motivated to Advance often find it difficult to be content with what they have. Instead, they might feel the need to move toward a future goal, something better or bigger that shows progress. This can create an aura of unrest in their life and make it difficult for others to be around them both professionally and personally.

THEY VALUE MOVING FORWARD MORE THAN GETTING IT RIGHT

At times, those with Advance as a top motivation value the need to check things off the list over the need to get those projects or tasks right. In other words, they are more concerned with efficiency than with effectiveness. For example, a content strategist for a nonprofit reflected to me that the leader of their organization was so focused on the next project, idea, or vision that he often missed important details and made halfhearted efforts in the work they were already doing. As a result, his team was constantly scrambling to execute his last idea, leading to a compromise of quality and lack of proper attention to work elements, which had to be redone later or did not reflect the organization's definition of excellence.

THEY ARE PRONE TO SEEING PEOPLE AS "MEANS" RATHER THAN "END"

In their attempt to hit their objectives, those driven to Advance might overlook the personal needs of their peers and collaborators and instead see them as merely a means to getting the work accomplished. When managing others, they might focus more on what a direct report can do for them than on that person's personal and professional development.

> **Four Things an Advance Person Might Say**
> - "Working every weekend this month? No big deal. We got it done!"
> - "What's next?" (before you've completed what's *now*)
> - "Close enough. Let's move on."
> - "Where is all this headed?" (perpetually focused on the future)

THEY CAN BE RELUCTANT TO DO MAINTENANCE ACTIVITIES

Because those driven to Advance need more and better opportunities, they might also pursue roles for which they are not yet equipped, even at the expense of the overall organization. Watch that their need to advance doesn't outstrip their preparedness for the role.

Working with a Motivated to Advance Person

HELP THEM CONNECT THE DOTS

A person who wants to make consistent progress needs a manager who understands this need and can help them connect what they are being asked to do with how it will help them meet their objective. Therefore, be very clear in how you address an Advance-motivated individual. Don't beat around the bush or explore things from multiple angles. If they get the sense you are wasting their time, they will do whatever they think is necessary to get the job done, even at the expense of themselves and others. But if they know you understand that their core drive is to Advance at all costs, they are more likely to trust in your leadership and listen to your advice.

CULTIVATE A SENSE OF MOMENTUM

Don't allow an Advance-motivated person to feel like things are stagnating. Create a sense of forward motion by setting expectations and establishing checkpoints that create frequent moments of accomplishment, and spend time explaining the sequence of events they must go through as they work on the project.

DON'T SETTLE FOR SUBSTANDARD WORK

At times, the Advance-motivated person will value moving on over excellence. As a manager, you can't allow them to put progress over quality work. Instead, help them understand what excellence looks like to you so they have a target to aim for, then hold them to that.

DON'T PROMOTE THEM TOO SOON OR BEYOND THEIR ABILITIES

Those motivated to Advance tend to be known as the go-getters within an organization, and are thus often handed the biggest and most challenging projects, regardless of whether they have the skills and abilities to execute them. Remember that an Advance-motivated person will often seek career opportunities before they are ready. Be patient with them, and make sure they are capable of performing the role for which you are considering them.

HELP SET THE CONTEXT

Those motivated to Advance will try to work around the system when they see it as inefficient—they might even skirt organizational protocol or existing processes by inventing their own. However, those processes might exist for a very good reason, so help them understand why certain systems are in place or why certain decisions have been made in the past. If they understand the context for the things they deem impediments, they are likely to be more tolerant when dealing with them.

Where They Thrive

ROLES WHERE PROGRESS IS MORE IMPORTANT THAN PRECISION

Those driven to Advance do best in environments that allow for quick execution: early-stage development, brainstorming, and startups with limited budgets. Because they are primarily motivated by forward momentum, any stalling to discuss details can eat away at their drive. Therefore, they are not well suited for roles requiring much regulation or in which making a wrong move can result in dire consequences, such as military leadership or surgery.

JOBS THAT REQUIRE RESOURCEFULNESS

Advance-motivated individuals don't wait around for someone to tell them how to do something—they just figure it out. As a result, they tend to prefer jobs that require them to learn new skills. However, don't expect them to master those skills. They will learn enough to get the job done, then move on to the next objective.

ROLES THAT CONCRETELY REWARD AMBITION

People motivated to Advance come alive when they have a clear path for advancement. They want to know how to get the next promotion, win the next client, or earn the next bonus, and once those guidelines are spelled out for them, they will pour themselves into their work until they accomplish their goal. But this can cause them to be perpetually discontent with where they are, which can have a negative effect on their engagement.

THE ACHIEVER FAMILY: SUMMARY

The person whose Motivation Code is made up of themes within the Achiever Family scales mountains. They are often the one who will accomplish the necessary work come hell or high water. If that's you, then it's likely you're someone always up for a challenge, and when one doesn't present itself, you'll create it. Here are a few final tips for you to consider as you plan your life and work:

Be Aware of Your Stress Level

You are probably tempted to take on too much at any one time. So be realistic about how much you can truly handle, and make sure you include regular periods of rest, recalibration, and interpersonal connection so you are not wearing yourself too thin in the pursuit of your goals. Remember that the priority is to sustain your productivity over a long period of time, not burn out far too soon. You are not a machine, so don't treat yourself like one.

Maintain Long-Term Goals, and Work toward Them Patiently

It might be tempting for you to lose sight of the long-term and more difficult-to-measure objectives in favor of shorter-term conquests. Keep a list of deeply personal, highly motivating goals and gauge your progress often to ensure you aren't sacrificing what matters most for the sake of tackling what matters now.

Don't Allow Your Ambition to Outpace Your Experience

It might be tempting to go after jobs or projects outside your current skill level and abilities. Your ambition is noble, but it's also wise to understand there is a time and place for everything. Be alert to moments you might be getting yourself in too deep. Find a few people who can help you discern which opportunities are right for you, and which ones you might not be ready for just yet. Understanding that you're not prepared isn't a failure on your part—it's wisdom.

Bring Others Along

In your effort to tackle big, impressive projects (which you will), don't forget to bring others along on the journey. Going solo is alluring because you only have to worry about your own goals and needs, but remember that the best work is almost always accomplished by teams, not solo practitioners. You need the perspective of others to sharpen your own efforts. Make certain you are building a collective of people to help you refine your vision, skills, and passion.

Chapter Five

THE TEAM PLAYER FAMILY

Common Characteristics

- Derives energy from working with others toward a common goal
- Is able to anticipate and meet the needs of others
- Willing to pick up extra work to help the team accomplish its objectives
- Wants to be part of something bigger than themselves, or part of an elite group

SOME PEOPLE ARE JUST *PEOPLE* PEOPLE. THEY WANT TO BE AROUND OTHERS, they love collaboration and interaction, and they come alive in meetings. They enjoy being involved in brainstorming sessions, and they always seem to show up energized and ready to go to team trainings. They are *team* people. They are more than happy to allow their teammates to shine. They don't always need the spotlight, and they're quick to praise others.

If your Motivation Code contains a theme within the Team Player Family, you likely pay close attention to others, especially in group contexts, and want to be involved with and contribute to the team's efforts. You might also derive energy from taking care of people, working to meet expectations, or influencing the behavior of others.

There are four key motivational themes within the Team Player Family:

1. Collaborate
2. Make the Grade
3. Serve
4. Influence Behavior

8: COLLABORATE

*You enjoy involvement in efforts in which
people work together for a common purpose.*

Watching my teenage daughter do homework is a wondrous thing. When I was in middle school, back when dinosaurs roamed the earth, I would lock myself in my room and just push through the assignments on my own until bedtime. If I didn't have an answer or know how to approach a problem, I would wait until I could ask the teacher the next day. My daughter, on the other hand, *never* does homework alone. She sits at the dining room table, FaceTiming with her friends. They don't share answers, but they help one another think about the work until they all arrive at solutions together. They each get to hear the others' perspectives on how to solve the problem, which makes them all more competent when the test rolls around. This is classic Collaborate behavior.

Unable to Win Unless the Group Wins

While those motivated by the Achiever Family of themes value individual accomplishments, those motivated to Collaborate focus most on the accomplishments of their work group. Many of their greatest moments involve team efforts, camaraderie, and overcoming obstacles together.

When they share their achievement stories, they say the word "we" frequently: "Then we . . ." or "We decided to . . ." They focus much more on what the team was able to do than on what they did uniquely.

Eager for Acceptance

The process of working together drives Collaborate-motivated people to excel, and their deepest satisfaction comes from knowing they are accepted as a part of the group, and that their individual contribution is important to the group effort. Again, it's not so much they are recognized externally as a great solo contributor, but that the group itself recognizes they are an important part of getting the work done.

Relationship Driven

Those driven to Collaborate are also great relationship builders. They seek to know the people they work with and are able to understand what they need in order to thrive. They are selfless, and will often give up what they want or need so that someone else on the team can flourish. They are very loyal and will defend their team publicly whenever they come under attack.

The Shadow Side

There are many positive qualities exhibited by people driven to Collaborate. However, their tendency to want to associate with a team or to do their work in the company of others can lead to a few shadow side attributes that must be managed.

THEY FIND IT EASY TO SELF-DEPRECATE

Those with Collaborate as a top motivation are often harder on themselves than they need to be and struggle to find their own worth separate from the team. They feel the need to downplay their successes so as not to overshadow the accomplishments of others. For this reason, they tend to struggle to represent their own interests or advocate for something they believe they deserve; they want to be a good team player.

THEY CAN LOSE THEIR INDIVIDUAL IDENTITY

People driven to Collaborate are much more likely to identify with a group than as an individual working within that group. Their personal sense of identity can become wrapped up in the team, which means their sense of self-worth can ebb and flow with the team's successes and failures. This can lead to very high highs, but also deep funks when things aren't going well. There are only so many aspects of the team dynamic within their sphere of control, so when they over-identify with the team it can lead to a sense that their life and career are being driven by others rather than their own internal compass.

THEY ARE PRONE TO TAKING ON TOO MUCH

Because Collaborate-motivated people are team players, they want to do their part. However, this can sometimes lead to taking on too much, to the point of burnout or subpar work. They are often the go-to person for tasks no one else wants to do, which may mean they are taking on more of the load than they should and aren't able to focus their efforts on the work they are uniquely capable of accomplishing.

THEY CAN JUDGE THOSE WHO ARE INDEPENDENT

Because they are so focused on the team's effort, they often don't understand those who are more motivated by personal achievement or recognition than the group's outcome. As a result, they might become judgmental toward those individuals, which can create conflict if not handled properly.

*THEY ARE RELUCTANT TO CONFRONT ISSUES
OR ENGAGE IN NECESSARY CONFLICT*

Those driven to Collaborate tend to avoid anything that might disrupt the team dynamic, so they refuse to engage in conflict, even when it is necessary or beneficial. However, this is simply not realistic in most organizations. Where there are talented, creative, driven people there will be conflict, simply because people bring their unique perspectives to the work. When disagreements arise, the Collaborate-motivated individual is likely to try to smooth them over or resolve them quickly, which may not be the best course of action.

Working with a Collaborate Person

INVEST IN YOUR RELATIONSHIP

Remember that the person motivated to Collaborate is less interested in the finish line and more interested in the process of getting there, especially as it relates to their interaction with others. Get to know them, and make sure you create an environment in which they feel you are working toward your team's goals together. Seek their input, and converse with them about their opinions, even when you initially disagree. Schedule team-building exercises with them, or invite them to lunch to discuss a project. It's important they feel welcomed into the decision-making process, even if their ideas aren't ultimately executed.

MAKE CONTRIBUTION A TWO-WAY STREET

While many managers are poised to be of assistance to their direct reports, those motivated to Collaborate need to feel they are contributing to the relationship as well. Seek ways to allow them to help you. Ask their opinion about important decisions you are making, or ask them to own elements of a project that will give them a sense that they are valuable to you. Ensure there is a give-and-take in your relationship with them.

ALLOW FOR MORE GROUP DISCUSSIONS THAN ONE-ON-ONES

While you want to ensure you're creating a personal relationship with those motivated to Collaborate, they often thrive in a group discussion. They feed upon the energy of the group, and tend to do their best thinking when responding to others' ideas. Consider how you might include a small group discussion into your team's workflow as a way to keep the Collaborate-motivated individuals energized.

PROBE ANY IDENTITY ISSUES

Pay special attention to areas where Collaborate-motivated people might be losing their sense of self because they are folding too readily into the team dynamic. If you sense an area where they seemed to disagree yet failed to speak their mind about their difference of opinion, ask them about it the next time you get the chance—although not in front of others. Ask them about their personal goals beyond the success of the team. Encourage them to stake a claim on their personal success rather than downplay their successes in favor of team recognition. While it's good to spread the praise, it's also important that team members learn to recognize themselves and each other for the great individual work they've done to contribute to the team's success.

Three Ways to Nurture a Team Player

- Identify a specific contribution they've made, and celebrate it with the team.
- Invite them into a small group discussion about an important topic, especially if it's a meeting they'd not normally attend.
- Allow them to choose their work group for a project.

HAVE HONEST CONVERSATIONS ABOUT CONFLICT

Those with Collaborate as a top motivation are prone to smoothing things over too quickly, which means that conflict is never truly resolved and only goes underground, until it erupts later in a more dangerous form. Therefore, teach them what constructive conflict resolution looks like, and help them understand the difference between healthy and unhealthy conflict. Unhealthy conflict is personal, whereas healthy conflict is about ideas and direction. Unhealthy conflict is about *being right*, whereas healthy conflict is about *getting it right*. Unhealthy conflict spans days or weeks; healthy conflict is acute, short-lived, and resolved quickly.

POINT OUT AREAS WHERE THEY ARE WORKING FROM OBLIGATION INSTEAD OF PASSION

Make sure you watch for areas where those driven to Collaborate are becoming overwhelmed with "gap work," tasks they squeeze into the gaps between their normal responsibilities, instead of spending their finite time and energy on things you're paying them to do. Yes, we all have to do work from time to time that we'd rather not, but those motivated to Collaborate take this to a new level by becoming the go-to person for tasks that would otherwise fall through the cracks.

Where They Thrive

HIGH-FUNCTIONING TEAMS

Those motivated to Collaborate are driven to work with others toward a common purpose, and they come alive when there is a high degree of trust and respect among team members. When a team is dysfunctional, they might take the burden upon themselves to try to make things better, which can lead to burnout. While they don't want to have to fix the team, they will make every effort to do so. However, when a team functions well, they feed off the collaborative energy and do their best, most satisfying work.

GROUP PROJECTS

These individuals are driven more by the interactions that lead to success than by individual recognition. Therefore, their motivation wanes when they have to work long hours on an individual element of a project. They function best when the work requires frequent check-ins, is developed together with others, or when their workspace allows them the ability to interact with teammates throughout the day, such as offices with open floor plans or that stay in constant communication with instant-messaging apps.

Jason is a mid-level manager of a financial services firm. While he never understood fully why, he seemed to go in and out of emotional funks throughout the course of the year and assumed it was just due to the seasons or the work he was required to do. During the first quarter of the year, his projects involved helping prepare the tax returns of dozens of clients. He was largely holed up in his workspace with little to no interaction with his team. The funny thing is, he actually *enjoyed* doing the tax returns. The work itself didn't bother him. In fact, he loved the puzzle-solving nature of it all. Over time he came to realize that the source of his funk was the isolation he experienced during those seasons. During the rest of the year, the entire team was involved in planning, client development, organizational brainstorming, and other types of highly social activity. Once tax season hit, it was all about cranking out the returns, which was mostly a solo endeavor.

Once Jason came to this realization, he was able to plan for tax season more appropriately. He would intentionally schedule social activities around his work, such as lunches with coworkers, strategically timed one-on-ones with his reports, and other types of interactive tasks that kept him at least marginally energized when the core work he was responsible for couldn't.

WORKING FOR A CAUSE

Because they want to be part of something bigger than themselves, Collaborate-motivated individuals often thrive when working for an organization pursuing something they consider worthy of their time and energy; it's beyond just collecting a paycheck. They want to be on a journey together with others, and nothing unites an organization like an ambitious cause.

9: MAKE THE GRADE

You are motivated to measure up to and gain acceptance into a group you want to be a member of.

Growing up, Scott wanted nothing more than to be an Eagle Scout, the most exclusive and difficult-to-achieve rank in the Scouts organization. Only about 6 percent of eligible Scouts earned the honor in 2018. Setting his mind on accomplishing his goal regardless of what it took, he spent nights and weekends earning merit badges, working on projects, and taking all the necessary steps to position himself to achieve Eagle Scout status.

Finally, after several years and a lengthy review process, Scott was awarded the rank of Eagle Scout shortly before his eighteenth birthday. For Scott, it wasn't so much the achievement itself that was most satisfying, but being accepted into the group. His motivation wasn't so much the process, but the ability to call himself an Eagle Scout, a group he would now be part of the rest of his life. Scott had Made the Grade.

Aware of What It Takes

Like Scott, those driven to Make the Grade want to measure up to social standards and meet the qualifications of groups they wish to join. They are driven to be recognized as having what it takes, and their internal motivation can ebb and flow depending on the level of acceptance they feel from the group.

Attracted to Groups with Standards

Their sense of status is often associated with belonging to a certain group. For this reason, they are often attracted to organizations whose participation is defined by measurable and high standards, such as the Scouts or the National Honor Society. In their work life, they want to be part of an organization that has clear standards for employees, such as graduation from prestigious schools or a minimum of experience to even get a job interview, and where they can feel pride in being a member of the team.

Team Oriented

Those driven to Make the Grade derive their greatest satisfaction from maintaining their position within the team. Just as with those motivated to Collaborate, Make the Grade–motivated people are likely to take on the work others don't want to do, and to be the "glue" that holds everything together when things get difficult. Many times, they'll subvert their personal goals for the sake of the team. At the same time, they are also team champions, singing the praises of their organization and its accomplishments. They are proud of the organization they associate with, and they are never shy about letting others know. As a result, their loyalty inspires others to bring their best, and helps teammates see that they also belong as part of the fold.

Defender of the Code

Finally, those with Make the Grade as a top motivation are zealous about standards and goals. They know what it takes to meet expectations, and they are often intolerant of those who don't seem to care much about standards. They protect the external perception of the team, and challenge others on the team to live up to it.

The Shadow Side

Those driven to Make the Grade are often the most committed and loyal members of your organization. With that, however, comes some potential shadow-side elements to be mindful of:

THEY ARE PRONE TO OVER-IDENTIFY WITH THE TEAM

As with those driven to Collaborate, it's often the case that those motivated to Make the Grade identify with the team and its goals to an unhealthy extent. For this reason, when they feel they are on the outs with team members or their manager, they can spin into destructive patterns of isolation, depression, and self-blame. In the same way, they can be excessively harsh with themselves when they fail to meet the standards of the team or organization.

THEY ARE WILLING TO PUT THE TEAM ABOVE THEIR OWN NEEDS

These individuals also tend to subvert their own health to accomplish their role on the team, even when it's not necessary. Because they tend to pick up the slack and spend all their available time doing whatever it takes to help the team succeed, it is easy for them to neglect sleep, eating, and exercise. There are situations when this is necessary, but for those motivated to Make the Grade, it's not an every-so-often thing—it's routine.

THEY LACK STRONG PERSONAL VIEWS

Those motivated to Make the Grade can unwittingly slip into groupthink, meaning they might lose their personal sense of vision and instead adopt the views and opinions of the team. As a result, they can often struggle to form their own opinions separate from those of the team leader or organizational vision.

THEY STRIVE TO STAY "QUALIFIED" AND "ACCEPTED" BY THE GROUP

If they sense that they might be falling out of favor with the group, they might overextend themselves in ways teammates find overbearing or cumbersome to deal with, such as needing constant affirmation that they belong, or oversharing their successes or credentials. They might continually ask "Was that okay?" or "How can I make this better?" even after being well within a project's success zone. They will also feel deeply hurt if they sense they are being excluded—socially or professionally—from the group. While this is the case for many people, these feelings are often much stronger for those driven to Make the Grade.

Working with a Make the Grade Person

One of the objectives when working with a person motivated to Make the Grade is to help them decouple their identity from the team's by encouraging them to recognize their own needs and wants. Here are a few ways to do this:

EXPLORE THEIR VALUES AND THE SOURCES OF THOSE VALUES

Ask them about the most important standards that guide their life and where they come from. Help them figure out what kinds of teams and standards help them function at their very best.

CONSIDER HOW MUCH TIME AND ENERGY THEY SPEND DOING THE WORK

Because they tend to conform to the group's needs, especially when doing so relates to acceptance, they can at times become overwhelmed with tasks at which they exhibit competence but not excellence. Therefore, it may be helpful to explore how much of their work is performed to stay in the good graces of their teammates versus how much is truly an expectation of their role.

MAKE THEM A PART OF YOUR TEAM

Establish shared standards that define your reporting relationship with them, and cultivate a sense that you're part of an exclusive team together by discussing the team's vision and what makes it special. Be very clear about expectations, and demand excellence from them. They will respond to the establishment of concise standards with deep engagement and productivity. Also, err on the side of including them in meetings or gatherings whenever possible. They want to feel like they are part of what's going on.

BE CONSISTENT

Those driven to Make the Grade are quite intolerant of hypocritical behavior. Therefore, they will lose respect for you if they sense you are not living up to the standards you or the team have set. Make certain your actions align with your words, and be open with the Make the Grade–motivated person when you fail to hit the mark.

AVOID INDIVIDUALISTIC BIAS

Throughout this section, we've cast a bit of a shadow on the idea of melding into a group or over-identifying with a team. It's true that when taken to extremes, this can lead to unhealthy behavior. At the same time, there can be a healthy and necessary aspect to this kind of loyalty, and you must be careful not to assume the worst. Yes, pay attention to areas where the Make the Grade–motivated person's behavior might drift into desperate clinging to the approval of the team or its mission, but also recognize that deeply loyal team members are often the ones who push projects across the finish line when others have given up hope. Reward this behavior while keeping your eye on areas where it might cross the line into burnout.

GIVE THEM SWAG

Those driven to Make the Grade often love to sport the team logo, to show their support and belonging. They will be the first to get the team T-shirt. Always include them in any initiative that allows them to show their connection to the team and its ideals.

Where They Thrive

ORGANIZATIONS THAT ARE DIFFICULT TO JOIN

Those motivated to Make the Grade want to know that they belong to an elite group, and are often drawn to organizations or teams that are the best of the best and regarded as very discerning about hiring. They don't just want to be in the Navy, they want to be a Navy SEAL, or better yet, a part of SEAL Team 6. They derive motivational energy from belonging to something they deem worthy of their life.

TEAMS WITH A STRONG CODE AND SENSE OF VALUES

Whatever organization they are a part of, it's important that those around them subscribe to a code defining how the team interacts and what's acceptable and what's not. If they sense hypocrisy within their leadership or teammates, they will begin to disconnect emotionally. However, if they see that everyone around them is striving to abide by a code, their sense of belonging and commitment to the organization will be fed. For this reason, people with Make the Grade as a top motivation are drawn to law enforcement, social work, academic work, and certain sectors of government work.

ORGANIZATIONS WITH A CLEAR REWARD STRUCTURE

It's important for Make the Grade–motivated individuals to know they are on course and their work is acceptable. When they go for long periods of time without feedback, it can be difficult for them to remain emotionally engaged. Therefore, they do best in organizations that offer frequent feedback; clear rewards for good work, such as recognition or praise for hitting the team's expectations; and an engaged manager committed to the development of the team.

10: SERVE

You are motivated to identify and fulfill needs, requirements, and expectations.

I worked with Pam for ten years. In that time, she was always on top of my schedule, and would remind me well in advance of anything she knew would affect my week, including big decisions I needed to make or deliverables others were expecting of me. She would also fend off unwanted distractions when I needed to go into "deep work" mode for a while. I always knew I could hand anything off to her and it would get done quickly and surpass my expectations. On top of it all, she was a great listener and helped me think through solutions to problems that were vexing me. Without her, I simply couldn't have survived.

Pam exhibits the attributes of the Serve motivational theme, but people with this as their top motivation can be found in every kind of role and organization, from the CEO who brings bagels to meetings and calls a team member whose mother is ill to the manager who thrives on mentoring and serving new recruits. At their heart, Serve-motivated people are passionate about meeting needs and advancing the cause of the team.

Quick to Spot What Is Needed

Those driven to Serve are motivated to identify and fulfill key needs, requirements, and expectations, and many are able to anticipate needs before they arise. They are often scanning the environment, looking for ways in which they can be helpful. This is especially true in times of crisis, when they will leap into action to ensure that everyone's needs are met.

Great Supporters

Those motivated to Serve are there to be of support to someone in need and to offer advice, information, and encouragement. They are often great listeners. They are the friend you call when you need a sympathetic ear, because you know they will be loyal, trustworthy, and there for you whatever it takes. They will almost always listen.

Go-To People

These individuals enjoy being the go-to person whenever something has to get done. They derive their motivational energy from being useful in whatever circumstances require their skills and effort. They are typically the person who volunteers to pick up coffee or clean up after an event.

Loyal

In this way, they are also extremely loyal to their organization, their team, their friends, their family, and their clients. They will be the person who's at your side when everything seems to be falling apart. They will keep your secrets. The cardinal sin for those driven to serve is betrayal of trust.

Willing to Go Above and Beyond

They are willing to go the extra mile to deliver results of a high standard. "Just good enough" is not enough for them. They want to please those whose expectations they are striving to meet, and will do whatever is necessary to over-deliver, especially when they haven't been asked to do so.

Focused on What's Right

They also typically have a focus on the greater good, and strive to serve a higher purpose. Their eye is on the organizational mission, and they scan for ways in which they might help to serve it. They can sometimes overstep their bounds, because they see something that needs to be done and simply step in and do it without asking for permission.

The Shadow Side

There are a number of watch points for those who derive their energy from meeting the needs of others:

THEY MAY NEED TO KNOW EXACTLY WHAT'S EXPECTED OF THEM AT ALL TIMES

The person driven to Serve wants to be useful, but sometimes precisely *how* to be useful is unclear. In those situations, they may not know how to behave or what to do until explicitly told. If there is a season in which they don't feel particularly useful, they might fall into an emotional slump or lose energy for their work. Or they might become overly communicative, seeking feedback frequently, even to the point it becomes distracting to everyone else on the team. They might seek personal approval from a manager at every turn, even over the most mundane tasks. The approval of the person they are serving is critical to their feeling like a success.

THEY ATTEND TO EVERYONE ELSE'S NEEDS, BUT NOT THEIR OWN

When your motivation is to serve others, it's easy to forget to take care of yourself. This is especially true in a fluid, fast-moving environment where there is an abundance of opportunity to serve. Those motivated in this way will sometimes lose sight of their own ambitions and desires, because they derive so much energy from ensuring that everyone around them has their needs met and nothing is falling through the cracks. However, this can lead to resentment and burnout over time if not monitored, or they can begin to feel animosity toward others if they feel taken advantage of, even though their actions were of their own choosing.

> **How a Person Motivated to Serve Can Care for Themselves**
>
> - Use your vacation days. (Yes, all of them.) If nothing else, it will prove that the world will go on without you.
> - Take time each day to be off the grid. It might be an hour before work in the morning or a quick, phone-free walk over lunch.
> - Commit to sharing your opinion at least once a day. It will remind you to use your voice, and that your perspective is valuable.

THEY CAN MEET NEEDS OTHERS DON'T WANT MET

Because they are always scanning the environment for opportunities, those motivated to Serve sometimes jump the gun and engage where their help isn't welcomed. While they believe they are simply being useful, to others this behavior can feel like meddling. They can also make things overly complex just to feel they are making progress on something, which can create tension among team members, who feel they aren't trusted to do their job. This makes it all the more important that those motivated to Serve ensure they have permission to act before jumping in to solve a problem.

THEY CAN ENABLE BAD BEHAVIOR

Because they are often very loyal, those motivated to Serve can get pulled into behavior that is less-than-ethical or simply counterproductive. So even when those they are striving to serve desire something that is unhealthy for them or that will work against their best interests, Serve-motivated people may still attempt to fulfill that wish.

THEY MAY BECOME MARTYRS

Those motivated to Serve can often feel taken advantage of, as if those they are serving aren't paying enough attention to the Serve individual's personal needs. If they feel ignored or overlooked, they might become bitter toward the team and organization, or become disruptive to the team dynamic. And surprisingly, they will often continue to do all the tasks they are motivated to handle in spite of this, all the while inwardly stewing over how they are being treated.

Working with a Serve Person

It's a true gift to have someone motivated to Serve on your team. They have a heart for getting things done, and they are likely to be the first person to volunteer for the job no one else wants. They take joy in producing value via responsibilities others shun. However, you also need to help them channel that beautiful motivation into work that is productive and healthy, and help them avoid ways in which this motivation might drift into self-defeating behavior. Here are a few tips:

CONSIDER HOW MUCH THEY'RE DOING

You might need to do regular check-ins to identify how much of a workload they are carrying at any given point. Because their tendency is to say yes even when they already have more than enough on their plate, those motivated to Serve can quickly become overwhelmed with discretionary work. Help them identify which responsibilities they can readily absorb versus which they should put on the back burner or shy away from to protect their time and energy.

HELP THEM IDENTIFY THEIR OWN NEEDS

Because their primary motivational energy comes from serving others, they might lose track of how well their own needs are being met. Have a conversation with them about areas where they feel they might be slipping into unhealthy patterns, not getting what they need in order to thrive, or feeling resentment toward others for possibly being overlooked or shortchanged. By helping them identify their needs and staying in touch with potential outages, you can keep ahead of conflict areas or burnout before it's too late or does a lot of relational damage.

CREATE A PLAN FOR SELF-CARE

Along with identifying their needs, help the Serve-motivated person develop a plan for self-care that allows them to continue to produce value for the organization over the long term. Suggest practices like the pursuit of personal goals, potential limits on work hours, and getting quality rest and exercise. While you want to avoid delving too deeply into their personal life, there is a tremendous correlation between whether someone cares for themselves and instances of workplace burnout.

ENCOURAGE THEM TO FIND ACCOUNTABILITY WITH THEIR TEAMMATES

It's not possible for you to be part of every interaction or monitor every decision the person makes, nor should you (or anyone) need to do so. However, it's often a good idea to encourage the Serve-motivated team member to find someone else in the group who can keep an eye on how many responsibilities they are taking on, and provide a bit of accountability if it seems they are absorbing too much. This accountability partner could also be a friend or loved one whom they check in with regularly to ensure they are staying healthy.

DIFFERENTIATE OPTIONS FROM OBLIGATIONS

When you are discussing their work with the Serve-motivated individual, carefully distinguish between ideas for next steps and actual tasks to be accomplished. Because they are motivated to meet needs, they might hear an idea as a request for action, and will jump in to accomplish it even absent of any request from you to do so. At the end of each meeting, ask them what their next steps will be so you are both clear about expectations and the amount of work they are tasked with. Always clarify expectations so they don't become artificially escalated in the Serve person's mind.

Where They Thrive

SUPPORT ROLES

Those driven to Serve come alive in jobs requiring them to anticipate the needs of a colleague and help them do their job more effectively. They might be a chief of staff or an executive assistant, or any role that makes someone else's life easier and more organized. They are primarily driven by knowing they've made someone else's burden a little lighter.

ORGANIZATIONS WHERE THEY ARE CLEARLY NEEDED

Those driven to Serve tend to scan the environment for any work that needs to be done or that might be falling through the cracks, so early-stage organizations like startups or new divisions being spun off from a larger organization, where team members have to do whatever is necessary to get the job done, are very motivating environments for them. They are likely to pick up any organizational slack and catch any dropped balls, and will find that deeply gratifying. They want to know that their service is appreciated, that needs they strived to meet are actually met. Response is often important to them. They want to know when they have hit the mark and satisfied the standards of others.

ROLES WITH CLEARLY DEFINED EXPECTATIONS

They enjoy being handed a task and a timeline—for example, planning a meeting for the entire team or figuring out the logistics of a video shoot. This is especially true when it's a task no one else wants to handle and their efforts would be the only way it will get done. Their greatest aspiration is to be of service to the cause, so they will rarely say no to these sorts of missions. However, they must be mindful of taking on too much and burning out.

11: INFLUENCE BEHAVIOR

You are motivated to gain a reaction or response from people that indicates you have influenced their thinking, feelings, and behavior.

"This is one of the worst nights of my life." Moments before, Terri had walked offstage after having delivered a speech she thought had bombed so completely it might just be the end of her career. All her usual jokes fell flat. There was no indication that any of her points were striking home with the room full of private bankers. Now she was sitting in a chair in the lobby, on the phone with her husband, trying to find some kind of solace in the midst of what was a certain disaster. "I just don't think I have it anymore," she said.

The session ended and people began pouring out of the auditorium into the lobby. Embarrassed, she immediately hung up the phone to make a quick escape before anyone saw her. It was too late. Several people approached her. One man quickly shoved a business card into her hand, saying he was the CEO of a large firm and wanted her to address his entire company at their annual meeting. Another was a conference organizer who wanted to discuss several events the following year. A woman revisited a point Terri had made in her speech and shared how much it had impacted her. Finally, the event planner told her how he had never seen such a response from this audience, and hoped that she would consider coming back in a few years.

After the throngs departed, Terri was left wondering what had happened. How could her impressions of her speech be so far off from the response she just experienced? How could a speech she thought had bombed have been one of the highlights of the event?

The reason Terri's gauge was so far off is that the primary motivation of her Motivation Code is Influence Behavior. Because the audience of private bankers was more subdued than she was used to, she wasn't getting the kind of feedback she needed to determine how she was performing. Despite the external cues, she was making a deep impact on the audience, and after receiving the feedback in the lobby, she returned home with a deep satisfaction that she'd done her job well.

Must See the Results of Their Influence

Those motivated to Influence Behavior are driven to gain a reaction or response from people that indicates the individual has influenced their thinking, feelings, or behavior. While many seek feedback from others, Influence Behavior–motivated people derive their primary motivational energy from seeing they have changed someone's ideas or behavior in some way. As a result, they tend to be very sensitive to the nuanced dynamics of behavior, and can read even the subtlest signs—a lack of eye contact, a small sigh, a sharp question—to determine whether their influence is breaking through.

Adept at Connecting with Others

They are capable of building strong relationships with a variety of people. They are often (though not always) extroverted, and draw energy from their interactions with others. They are able to relate to people from a wide variety of backgrounds, and are typically not intimidated by meeting new people—it's an opportunity to make an impression. They also often exhibit a high degree of empathy, and are able to understand and share the feelings of others. Because they are highly attuned to how a person responds to their words and actions, they pick up on social cues that others miss, like amount of eye contact or posture, whether the person is leaning forward or nodding along. This often makes them more capable of saying or doing just the right thing at the right moment to ease a situation. They know how to reach each kind of "audience" with just the right touch to leave their mark.

The Shadow Side

Those motivated to Influence Behavior are often driven by the response they perceive in others. This can have some shadow-side effects:

THEY OVERVALUE WHAT OTHERS THINK OF THEM

Like Terri at the beginning of this section, those motivated to Influence Behavior are often overly attuned to the opinions of others, and can go into a tailspin, shut down emotionally, and even withdraw from the group entirely when they believe they are not making the impression they desire.

THEY LOOK FOR RESPONSES AT THE WRONG TIME AND PLACE, OR TOO FREQUENTLY

Because Influence Behavior–motivated people are wired for frequent feedback, they often seek it anywhere they can find it. However, not every situation is appropriate for a feedback session. The desire for input about their performance can hinder the natural working rhythms of a team and become a burden on their manager or teammates.

*THEY CAN EXPERIENCE HIGHS AND LOWS
BASED ON HOW THEY'RE RECEIVED*

Those with Influence Behavior as a top motivation tend to be ruled by feelings. If they have had a few bad experiences recently, it can affect their emotional engagement at work. They can also allow their emotions to have more influence over their interactions with teammates than is appropriate, and they might overextend themselves to try to gain a response from them, even when the timing is inappropriate. For example, they might hide in a corner if no one is interested in their story at a dinner party, or withdraw from engaging if their idea isn't received well in a meeting.

Working with an Influence Behavior Person

When working with someone motivated to Influence Behavior, you need to seek ways to connect deeply and personally, and to show them you are interested in their perspectives and ideas. They are driven to have impact on you and the team, so you provide an avenue for doing so.

BE EXPRESSIVE AND ENGAGING

It's important when managing someone motivated to Influence Behavior that you show them how they are impacting your thinking and feelings. They will respond to your engagement with their ideas, and might interpret a stoic posture as disinterest in them or their thoughts. Do your best to respond both verbally and with your body language to show you are interested in what they are saying. Lean forward. Smile and nod. Ask good questions. Meet with them in person or by video call, not by phone or text. This might seem obvious, but they will respond better to your leadership and ideas if they can see you during the conversation, because much of how they internalize information and respond to ideas is driven by the nonverbal feedback they receive. Make every attempt to avoid conference or one-on-one calls when possible.

ALLOW YOURSELF TO BE INFLUENCED

Don't take an argumentative posture out of the gate. Show that you are willing to entertain their ideas, even if you believe they are wrong. Reveal to them when your mind is changing because of their influence, even if they don't completely alter your thinking.

ENCOURAGE THEM TO DEVELOP SELF-AWARENESS AND SELF-REGULATION

Because their emotions and engagement are often deeply affected by how others are receiving their ideas, they can lose sight of their own sense of self and personal ambitions. Help them identify their goals and establish markers of personal excellence that are separate from the feedback of others. Of course, this is a tricky line to walk, especially because many of those motivated to Influence Behavior are "performers" at heart, and the audience fuels their drive to be excellent. The key is to help them decouple from the perceived negative responses and instead focus on whether they performed their role with excellence and commitment.

MAKE CONNECTIONS BETWEEN THEIR BEHAVIOR AND THAT OF THEIR ROLE MODELS

Those who are driven to Influence Behavior are also often driven to be influenced by those they admire. There can be a deep connection between the ideas and behaviors of the people they look up to and their personal choices in their work. Ask them frequently about their influences and whom they admire most. Ask them to discuss the people in their life who have held the most sway over their decisions and career. Talk about ways in which their thinking has been shaped by the people they look up to. This can increase their level of self-awareness, and also help them understand how they may have adopted behavior—even unknowingly—from others, whether healthy or unhealthy.

> **Three Ways to Encourage a Person Motivated to Influence Behavior**
>
> - Share something specific they said that caused you to change your mind.
> - Thank them for their insightful comments at the end of a meeting.
> - Invite them to lunch and seek their advice about a decision you're trying to make.

Where They Thrive

HIGH-PROFILE COMMUNICATION ROLES

Those motivated to Influence Behavior often thrive in positions where they are tasked with communicating new ideas, or where they have the chance to change minds about an important topic. Roles such as speaking, being the point person on company presentations, and high-visibility leadership are perfect for them. They enjoy being the presenter of new work or the lead on pitching ideas to a client. They want to be the one who drives the point home. Of course, the downside of these roles is that the Influence Behavior person's motivation can wax and wane depending on the response they receive from the audience.

ON A STAGE

Those motivated to Influence Behavior draw energy from a crowd of onlookers. Therefore, they often do well in roles where the primary objective is to entertain, such as acting or music. They are highly attuned to what it takes to win over a skeptical audience or get a laugh at the right moment. They are skilled at morphing into whatever they need to be to develop empathy and sway someone's perspective.

TEACHING OR TRAINING

Almost any job with an element of teaching or training will bring gratification to the person driven to Influence Behavior. The immediate feedback and ease with which their impact can be measured are likely to draw them into these categories of professions. Schoolteachers, corporate trainers, professors, and HR/learning and development specialists who love their work likely have this theme in their Motivation Code.

THE TEAM PLAYER FAMILY: SUMMARY

If you are motivated by a Team Player theme, here are a few tips for structuring your life and work for maximum effectiveness:

Have a Clear Set of Personal Values That Guide Your Decisions

As mentioned throughout this chapter, you are likely very loyal and willing to fold into the organizational effort when needed. However, it's critical that you have a clear set of personal values and beliefs that ground you so you don't get lost in everyone else's priorities.

Monitor Your True Stress Level

You have broad shoulders. You are capable of taking on far more than others are willing to attempt. However, this means you might be tempted from time to time to take on too much. Make certain you have frequent self-check-ins to ensure your stress level is healthy and you aren't overextending yourself. Make a commitment to take certain days off, and keep it. (Don't even check your email, or you'll be tempted to jump into the conversation or take on a task.)

Be Mindful of How the Opinions of Others Might Be Influencing Your Mood

Often, Team Players are deeply influenced by how others in their environment react to their ideas and presence. If you find yourself frustrated, evaluate how much of your mood is attributable to external forces versus internal ones. Did someone ignore your idea in a meeting? Is your relationship with a coworker souring? Are you feeling taken for granted by the rest of the team, unnoticed for your efforts? Spend some time thinking or journaling about these factors and how they might be impacting your ability to engage.

Shamelessly Champion the Causes You Believe In

One of the great attributes of the Team Player is their loyalty to what they believe in—you are a great ambassador! Choose your causes, and don't be shy about standing up for them. You will be at your most fulfilled when you are attached to a cause bigger than yourself and working alongside others who believe they are making a difference in the world. If you ever find yourself in an emotional lull, consider whether it might have something to do with a lack of a cause to champion.

Brilliant work is most often accomplished by teams of people stumbling forward into uncertainty and trying to figure things out as they go. This requires a lot of trust and a high degree of commitment, to one another and to the work. In this kind of environment, the Team Player becomes an invaluable resource. They are often the glue that holds the effort together. They are there to champion the team's values, and to ensure that it never loses sight of the big picture.

Chapter Six

THE LEARNER FAMILY

Common Characteristics

- Motivated to explore, ask questions, and learn new things
- Driven to teach others what they've learned and share new skills
- Prefers generalist roles
- Able to bring a lot of new ideas and energy to projects, especially in the early stages

THOSE WHOSE MOTIVATION CODE IS MADE UP OF THEMES WITHIN THE Learner Family are usually motivated to explore and learn new things, gain mastery, and demonstrate their knowledge. When beginning a new venture or engaging in work requiring deep, domain-specific knowledge, they are excellent collaborators. They are also almost always willing to shoulder the burden of diving into complex issues and figuring things out.

There are four motivational themes within the Learner Family:

1. Comprehend and Express
2. Master
3. Demonstrate New Learning
4. Explore

12: COMPREHEND AND EXPRESS

Your motivation focuses on understanding, defining, and then communicating your insights.

Did you know that Abraham Lincoln would walk for miles just to borrow a single book? As the son of a rural farmer, he had little access to reading material, so he would borrow one book at a time from neighbors, often trekking many miles over heavy terrain just to get his hands on a desired tome. Although Lincoln didn't take the Motivation Code assessment, as this example shows, those motivated to Comprehend and Express gravitate to tasks that involve research, deep thought, learning in new areas, exploring models, or connecting dots. It doesn't matter how obscure the topic might be, they have a story that connects the dots and offers clarity.

Eager to Share What They've Learned

Those motivated in this way are driven to understand, refine, and communicate their insights. They are at their best and most energized when absorbing new concepts and turning extremely difficult and conceptual ideas into something easily absorbable by others. Learning, to them, is a continual activity. They can spend much of their day lost in a deep thought. However, all this learning is not just for its own sake. They also want to express their ideas to others in a useful way. This is an equally important aspect of this motivation: an insight is not nearly as motivating if they aren't able to find a channel with which to express it. In fact, they might feel as if their comprehension is incomplete unless it is put into some kind of expression. They often learn as they teach ideas to others, working out their thoughts publicly. For this reason, these individuals tend to be great teachers, and will over time make their way into roles that allow them to instruct others.

Able to Connect the Dots

Those driven to Comprehend and Express like to explore a wide variety of subjects and make connections among them. They also deal well with complexity and make sense of ideas that others find too obtuse or challenging. They will spend the time necessary to comprehend the issues and forge connections with their already vast set of insights. If they don't immediately grasp an idea, they will stay with it as long as they need to in order to feel they've mastered it. Then they will simplify and share it with others.

Specialists

Though they often have a wide-ranging knowledge of various subjects, they also often center on one or a few areas to dive deeply into and explore. Because of this, it's not uncommon that they have an extensive understanding of their primary field of interest, even if it's not directly related to their job.

The Shadow Side

While they are often the source of new ideas and stimulating conversation, there are a few shadow-side attributes that those driven to Comprehend and Express must be mindful of:

THEY MAY BECOME PARALYZED BY OVERTHINKING

Because they tend to live in their head, it's easy for those motivated to Comprehend and Express to spend too much time considering options and exploring ideas. They can get lost in a subject and not reach the expression stage, which only creates internal tension, as they feel they are not achieving their full, true motivation.

THEY CAN BE INDECISIVE

In the same way, it's easy for them to get lost in the weeds and fail to make critical decisions at the right time. Quick decisions can be difficult for them because they need to understand all sides of a problem before they are willing to progress. This can be frustrating to fellow team members who are motivated to move forward and finish the project quickly.

THEY CAN COME ACROSS AS A KNOW-IT-ALL

They are often the first to speak up on topics they know well, and their conversation can at times feel like a side note to the subject at hand because they see a connection that no one else does. As a result, they can come across as intellectually arrogant, or as if they believe they are superior in their insight and knowledge. They don't intend this, but it's how some who are less secure about their abilities might perceive their generous sharing of information.

THEY CAN BE IMPRACTICAL

Those driven to Comprehend and Express fail to make the necessary practical connections between their ideas and the real world. They might pontificate about some loose connection between two experiences or ideas and expect everyone else to get excited along with them, only to realize that most of the people in the room are simply waiting for them to get to the point. They might seem aloof or disconnected from the team or the work because they are playing with ideas, or it might take them a while to land back in a place where they can meaningfully communicate their thoughts to everyone else. They can be accused of making things too complex, especially when they haven't had the time to really sort through their thoughts and do the deep work of synthesis. However, once they are given the opportunity to do so, they often come out on the other side with a wonderfully elegant explanation or recommended course of action.

THEY CAN CREATE UNNECESSARY HURDLES FOR TEAM PROGRESS

They can also create hurdles in the later stages of a project. For example, research manager Joe preferred to explore the wide-open spaces of the work rather than complete tasks. "We would be in the late stages of the project," he says, "and I would start asking things like 'What if we look into . . . ?' or 'Have we investigated . . . ?' I would push the team to go back into the idea phase of the project." This created tension because the project was well beyond the stage where those kinds of questions were useful. Because he was the team leader, others would follow his instincts, even though they weren't what was best in the moment. Once he realized how his motivation was derailing his work, he was able to scale back and wrap up the project.

THEY TEND TO GROW BORED WITHOUT NEW CHALLENGES

If they are in a season of execution, with little opportunity to explore and learn, those driven to Comprehend and Express have a tendency to shut down, get bored, or spend their time in ways that aren't immediately helpful to the organization. They might begin a new research project or explore other ideas, which means they aren't focused on helping the team accomplish its immediate goals. They might also become disruptive in meetings, asking questions ancillary to the main issue or that use the team's precious time on matters not relevant at the moment.

THEY TEND TO SHARE IDEAS BEFORE THEY'RE READY

Because they are motivated to share ideas with others, they are sometimes tempted to share them before they're fully baked. If this happens too often, it can result in a loss of credibility or lead the team in unhelpful directions as they work out their ideas in public. For this reason, they might need someone in their life to routinely bounce ideas off before sharing publicly.

Working with a Comprehend and Express Person

To connect with these individuals, it's best to create space for them to share their opinions.

TEACH AND LEARN

Provide opportunities for learning and development, such as reading materials, seminars, workshops, courses, and conferences. Take time to teach them not only what works, but also *why* it works, to satisfy their curiosity. Also, be open to being instructed by them when they want to teach you something. Be open-minded and allow them to express their insights, even when you don't see the immediate connection to the topic at hand.

PREPARE FOR (AND BE PATIENT WITH) QUESTIONS

Understand that they will want to explore all aspects of a project before diving in, and they will likely be full of questions at the outset. Be patient with them, and know that their questions are not a function of distrust, but of their deep desire to delve into the nuances of something before taking the first steps. Encourage them to ask questions, and reward their curiosity with verbal feedback, especially in front of the team. Also, draw clear boundaries about what you can and can't share at any moment: "I'm sorry, but we're not ready to discuss that yet" is perfectly acceptable to them, as long as they know the time will come to scratch that curiosity itch.

BE TOLERANT OF LAPSES IN EMOTIONAL SENSITIVITY

Because they often live in their head, those motivated to Comprehend and Express can sometimes lack the social graces or emotional intelligence necessary to function in a healthy way within a team environment. Watch for moments when this exhibits itself (for example, talking over someone else in a meeting to share their idea), and coach them through better handling of those situations moving forward. Teach them how to allow the other person to finish, compliment their insight, then share their own, building on the other person's idea whenever possible. Help them understand that developing an intuitive, empathetic posture can broaden their ability to comprehend and share their ideas with others. And know that they don't intend to be rude or disconnected—it's just an aspect of their motivation.

WATCH OUT FOR ANALYSIS PARALYSIS

Are they stuck because they are spending too much time in one minor area of a much bigger project? Are they spinning their wheels trying to connect two dots that don't really need to be connected? Talk to them about their thought process, and if necessary, direct them toward other, more critical problems that need to be solved. Make sure they are spending their finite mental faculties on the most important elements of a project rather than spinning out on the minutia.

In the same way, you can help them understand that moving forward—even without all the information they believe they need—can be in itself a learning experience. Talk to them about next actions and how they plan to make progress on their project. Work through timelines and detailed schedules so they clearly understand expectations.

ASSIGN THEM RESEARCH PROJECTS

Do you have something on the horizon that needs research and organization? Assign it to them, and give them plenty of time to get ahead of it. While sitting with resource materials and combing through complex ideas can feel like a burden to some of your team members, those motivated to Comprehend and Express will see it as a huge gift. Also, know that they are likely among the best people to invite into a brainstorming session, as they will bring a wealth of stimulus to the table. However, stay mindful of their tendency to be a little too much in their head and how that could affect the practical execution of the project.

> **Three Ways to Engage a Comprehend and Express Person**
>
> - Ask them to do a study on trends in your industry and report their findings back to the team.
> - Assign them to begin thinking of ideas for a project the team will undertake in two months. Let them get ahead of you.
> - Over coffee or lunch, ask them to share what they've been reading or learning.

Where They Thrive

TEACHING AND TRAINING

Similar to those driven to Influence Behavior, those driven to Comprehend and Express find teaching and training roles deeply gratifying because they provide the opportunity to learn new things and routinely share them with others. However, unlike Influence Behavior, which is mostly about how the individual's work impacts other people, it's important that Comprehend and Express–motivated individuals have the ability to absorb a wide range of new information and are not simply teaching the same curriculum over and over. If they are put in a position where they are simply regurgitating the same information in session after session, or semester after semester, they might lose interest. For example, if they are a college professor, the initial stages of compiling and delivering a curriculum will find them right in their motivational sweet spot, but once they've delivered the material a few times they will begin to lose their drive.

RESEARCHING AND WRITING

Jobs that allow them to get out ahead of everyone else and survey new territory, then report back what they've discovered, are ideal for those driven to Comprehend and Express. So research and development, authoring books, creating media that helps others understand important topics, or writing reports or white papers on new ideas and trends will be deeply satisfying to them.

INNOVATIVE WORK

They love to connect dots and share new insights and ideas, so any job that allows them to intuit new paths for an organization or client, then share those insights with them in a practical way, are likely to resonate. They make excellent creative team leaders, marketing specialists, or idea generation leads, as they are always looking for what's new or trending.

13: MASTER

Your motivation is satisfied when you gain complete command of a skill, subject, procedure, technique, or process.

In 2020, the world lost a true music icon when Neil Peart, drummer for the rock band Rush, died. Widely touted as one of the greatest drummers and percussionists in history, Peart was an idol to musicians around the world. What many people don't know is that he continued to take drum lessons well into his career, even after he was considered one of the greatest of all time. In a 2012 interview, he told *Rolling Stone* magazine, "What is a master but a master student? And if that's true, then there's a responsibility on you to keep getting better and to explore avenues of your profession. I've been put in this position, and I certainly don't underrate that. I get to be a professional drummer."

In just a few sentences, Peart perfectly summarized the mind-set of the person motivated to Master.

Mastery over Knowledge

Those motivated to Master are satisfied when they gain complete command of a skill, subject, procedure, technique, or process. They love to dive deeply into a niche subject until they are intimately familiar with its nuances. Their drive to learn is persistent, whether it's a topic area, a skill, or a discipline. To them, it's not about public recognition—it's about their personal sense of perfecting their craft.

It's All in the Details

Detail is important to those motivated to Master, and execution of the most intricate parts of a process or skill matter. If they miss one small piece, it can frustrate them to no end, and they might feel the desire to go back to the beginning and start over.

Perfectionists

Those driven to Master tend to see perfection as the ultimate goal. They hold themselves to a very high, and often unrealistic, standard and have a hard time allowing subpar performance. While this perspective can be harmful, it is also what allows them to measure their efforts and know they are on course. For example, a competitive runner might significantly improve her time in a race, but if her strategy wasn't executed flawlessly, she might still struggle to find gratification in her performance. However, the combination of high performance and flawless execution provides fuel for her to continue striving to reach the next goal.

Top Performers

As a result, Master-motivated people tend to be the virtuosos of their respective fields. They are the ones setting the standard of excellence.

They are typically also specialists rather than generalists. They are masters of a very select set of skills rather than being relatively good at a lot of things. They strive to be the first person called when their particular skill set is needed.

Hard Workers

Finally, they tend to be hardworking and diligent, and they will do whatever it takes to be successful in their field and feel the gratification of being a master. They usually set their life up around the practice of their craft, and seek others who can help them become better. They will hire coaches, read all the latest literature in their field, and take on far more than everyone else. Again, they don't engage in this behavior for public recognition, but because of their innate desire to be great at what they do.

The Shadow Side

While their commitment to excellence and drive toward perfection can yield remarkable results for themselves and the organization, there are some key watch points the person driven to Master must keep an eye on to ensure their compulsion to pursue excellence isn't getting in the way of their ability to consistently produce great work:

THEIR SENSE OF PERFECTIONISM CAN LEAD TO
PERPETUAL DISSATISFACTION

While it's great to strive for high performance, those driven to Master can sometimes allow that instinct to cross into unhealthy behavior. They might find it difficult to enjoy any activity because they are never satisfied with their execution. They look for all the flaws, and spend a lot of time and resources eking out that final percent of performance when no one else understands why they aren't happy with the way things are. This perfectionism can manifest as anger at themselves and occasionally others.

THEY OFTEN FAIL TO ACT BECAUSE THE "REHEARSAL" DIDN'T GO WELL

If those with Master as a top motivation don't believe they are ready for prime time, they might be hesitant to jump into a project or performance. They believe they have to get it exactly right before they engage in any public way. For example, an executive rehearsing a speech to a group of investors might work for weeks to perfect the language of the speech, and if she doesn't feel her rehearsal is perfect, might seek ways of delaying the presentation until she feels she's ready. Their high standards are difficult to meet, which means they never feel as if something is ready to be experienced by others.

THEY TEND TO GET LOST IN THE DETAILS

In their attempt to squeeze just a little more performance out of their effort, they can sometimes lose sight of the bigger picture. For example, a writer who wants desperately to get a sentence or two right might spend days perfecting the language of that one small section while ignoring the fact that she is under deadline to deliver an entire manuscript. Those small, imperfect details can haunt the person driven to Master, and they can lose sight of the grand objective. Because of this, they can be much slower than everyone else around them, and can't always be relied upon to get things done in a timely manner.

THEY MIGHT DRIVE THEMSELVES AND OTHERS TOO HARD

Their commitment to excellence can make them challenging to work with. They may push the team to wring the last bit of value out of a client or project, and they are rarely satisfied with the results until their personal standard of excellence is satisfied, regardless of what the client or organization wants. Also, because their standard of excellence is highly personal and subjective, they might struggle to communicate their expectations to their team, and instead rely on an "I'll know it's right when I see it" approach.

Working with a Master Person

**HELP THEM DISTINGUISH BETWEEN
WHAT CAN AND CANNOT BE MASTERED**

The key to working with a person motivated to Master is to help them identify the areas in which they should strive to pursue mastery, and those in which perfection is more harmful than helpful. Often, getting something 90 percent right and moving on is more valuable to the organization than squeezing out that final 10 percent. At the end of the day, there are some skills that simply cannot be mastered for a variety of reasons: how a client responds to an idea, general market or economic trends, or even one's own limitations.

What can be mastered	What can't be mastered
Your sales technique	Whether a client buys
Your stage presence	Whether an audience responds to your presentation
Your design technique	Whether your manager likes the idea
Your ability to craft a strategy	Unseen forces that determine its success or failure

POINT OUT WHEN THEY ARE SPREAD TOO THIN

Their desire to specialize and Master a number of skills can cause them to take on too much, and their plate can fill up very quickly. Ask them questions about their present workload, where they are spending their time, anticipated timelines for particular projects, and any areas of frustration they are currently experiencing. Help them diagnose the source of their frustration, and identify areas where they are getting too far into the weeds or striving to master something that doesn't need to be mastered.

DON'T PROMOTE THEM BEYOND THEIR ABILITIES

Because of their drive to be excellent, those motivated to Master can stand out early in their career. However, perfecting a set of skills is a very different thing from managing others performing those skills. As their role becomes more complex and their responsibilities encompass more uncertain kinds of work, like strategy and decision making, they can begin to stall as they strive to understand every nuance of a situation, or try to perfect every strategy. In these situations, they can cause frustration for the team, who are really just trying to get the work done but feel their manager has now become a roadblock. Before promoting the person motivated to Master into a managerial role, make certain they understand the nature of the work, and make sure to stay in constant contact with them about their process, decisions they are considering, and their timelines for execution.

TAKE CHARGE OF THE DETAILS

If they sense that your commitment to excellence is lacking, you might lose their respect. Strive to pay attention to the details, because they certainly will be. You don't have to be perfect, but you must be organized and detailed enough in how you lead and communicate that they will respect your management. If they are on your team, understand that they might get sidetracked during a project as they attempt to perfect the work. They might rewrite a single paragraph in a report a dozen times when "close enough" would be perfectly fine. Don't be afraid to say, "I think it's great the way it is. Thanks for your hard work on this." Also, recognize areas where they are exhibiting excellence as a peer, for example when you notice they led a meeting well or did all the right prep work for a call with a client.

Where They Thrive

HIGH-STAKES ROLES

Many people motivated this way are drawn to roles that allow continual perfection of their skills, especially if those skills are rare and valuable. Any role that requires precision is attractive to them, while roles that are "get it in the ballpark and move on" in nature will be less satisfying. For example, you want your surgeon to be motivated to Master because the threshold for mistakes is small and the stakes are so high.

OPEN-ENDED TIME FRAMES

Those driven to Master will often work on something right up to the deadline, trying to get it just right. They might get lost in the details and fail to deliver on the core objective because they were trying to tweak the finer points. So any work that is open-ended and allows for continual improvement will be gratifying, while tasks with pressure-packed timelines requiring "good enough" performance will not satisfy them.

DETAILED WORK

Those driven to Master prefer jobs allowing them to dive deep into topics that others might gloss over. Need someone to thoroughly understand that new contract? They're your person. Want someone to look through every stage of your new process to make certain there aren't any oversights? Give them some time to do it, but they won't rest until they know it's perfect.

14: DEMONSTRATE NEW LEARNING

You are motivated to learn how to do something new and show that you can do it.

Jim was a serial hobbyist. He had a history of learning a new skill, wowing others with it, and then moving on to some other interest. When he decided to take up gardening, his wife was thrilled—she'd always dreamed of having a vegetable garden. For one season, the garden did great. Jim was routinely in their backyard working on the plants, and he would share all his new techniques around the dinner table or at parties. However, when the next spring rolled around, the garden lay dormant. Planting season passed, and Jim was only in the backyard once. Instead, he was spending most of his time in the garage. He'd moved on to another hobby: fixing bicycles.

Jim's most prominent motivational theme is Demonstrate New Learning. This means he is motivated to develop knowledge or skill in an area, then demonstrate that proficiency to other people. It's not enough for Jim to simply learn a skill if there isn't the accompanying second component of demonstration. However, once he has developed the new skill and demonstrated it to others, he is ready to move on and learn something new.

Quick Learners

Those motivated to Demonstrate New Learning are often adept at developing skills as quickly as possible. But complete mastery of a skill or understanding of a topic is not important to them—they simply want solid proficiency without pressing toward mastery. For this reason, they might show off their skills before they are fully ready to do so.

Generalists

These individuals tend to be generalists: they spend their time learning how to do a little bit of everything, and are always looking for opportunities to utilize their "Swiss Army knife" skill set. The idea of specializing in just a few core areas is unappealing, as they would much rather play a large number of roles in life and work. Unlike those motivated to Comprehend and Express, those motivated to Demonstrate New Learning tend to be much more practical and action oriented, seeking skills they can immediately put into practice. To them, practical application is more important than an idea.

Strong Synthesizer

Demonstrate New Learning–motivated people have strong communication skills. Because they don't get caught in the nuances of a skill set or topic area, they are able to simplify topics for others and give them the big picture.

The Shadow Side

Because they have so many interests and are often wired to be a generalist, those driven to Demonstrate New Learning can exhibit a few shadow-side attributes:

THEY FIND IT DIFFICULT TO COMMIT TO A CAREER

Because they quickly gravitate to learning and acquiring new skills, they often find it difficult to commit and follow one path wholeheartedly. As a result, they might bounce from job to job, and are likely to quit when something more appealing comes along. They might want promotion simply for the sake of a new challenge. However, as soon as they feel proficient enough in that role, they'll begin their search for the next job.

THEY ARE A JACK-OF-ALL-TRADES AND MASTER OF NONE

Those motivated to Demonstrate New Learning tend to know a little about everything, and a lot about very little. In some settings, such as the early stages of a startup, this can be valuable because they can shoulder many responsibilities. However, as the organization grows and more specialization is required, they can often find themselves in the awkward position of not wanting to get locked into one area of expertise, which can make them difficult to slot within the team's structure.

THEY MAY COME ACROSS AS A KNOW-IT-ALL

Although unintentional, those driven to Demonstrate New Learning can come across as show-offs. Due to their multitude of proficiencies, they are quick to chime in and share information or correct someone in a conversation, even if it's unwanted. At parties, they have a story or factoid about every subject, and can often relay a personal experience to bolster their authority. Ultimately, they must learn to discern when it is appropriate to make such comments and when this behavior is uncalled for.

THEY WANT TO APPEAR COMPETENT, EVEN WHEN THEY AREN'T

These individuals tend to rush in and share something they have just learned well before others are ready to hear it. For example, a businessman shared that as a child he'd decided to teach himself how to do ventriloquism. He'd spent about thirty minutes working on a routine, then proudly announced to the teacher on Monday that he would like to share his new act with the classroom. As you can imagine, his skill was not nearly sufficient, but that didn't bother him. It was more about sharing what he'd learned over the weekend.

Working with a Demonstrate New Learning Person

ENCOURAGE THEM TO JUGGLE MULTIPLE TASKS

The one certain way to lose a Demonstrate New Learning–motivated individual's heart and mind is to stick them in a role where they're doing the same tasks daily with no end in sight. When possible, find ways to give them multiple responsibilities that require them to learn new skills and explore new disciplines. Allow them to operate across multiple teams or sit in on group brainstorms. If there's a project that will require a bit of research, allow them to go out and learn what they can, then report back to the team. The more diverse their job description, the more likely you are to get the best out of them. However, know that even with many tasks, they might still grow bored once they've achieved a sufficient level of proficiency. At that point, you might need to actively manage them to ensure they don't "tinker" their way into areas where they don't belong. However, if you are able to keep them engaged and stimulated, they will reward you with brilliant work.

ENLIST THEIR HELP ONLY WHEN YOU'RE READY

Because those motivated to Demonstrate New Learning are usually looking for new things to learn, they will often leap into a task with both feet before you're ready for them to do so. Therefore, establish clear timelines for their work, and only introduce projects once you're ready for them to engage. Otherwise, they might get too far ahead of you and the rest of the team.

HELP THEM IDENTIFY OPPORTUNITIES FOR GROWTH

Because they are competent in so many areas, it can be hard for them to see where they lack the necessary skills to thrive. Their ability to dive in and become competent in an area quickly creates a bit of a false sense of overall mastery. For this reason, help them identify and understand opportunities for growth, and put a concrete plan in place to either help them develop those skills or to avoid certain tasks for which they are not yet qualified.

ADDRESS THE CHALLENGE OF INSTABILITY

They will likely lose interest in a role or new project once they've achieved a level of proficiency, and will begin looking for a new challenge to tackle. Help them see when this is happening so they stay focused and engaged with the work even when their motivation is waning. One way to do this is to point them to side projects that need attention and can allow them to explore and grow their skills. Having an outlet for this motivation will make the day-to-day work much more possible.

TEACH THEM HOW TO TEACH

If they are able to redirect their need for new challenges to the role of developing other people, they will find a never-ending supply of fresh stimulus and ideas to fuel their motivation. Provide them with opportunities to demonstrate their skills to the team, and when appropriate, to teach others how to do what they do. Also, allow them to teach you. They flourish when they can share their interests.

Where They Thrive

GENERALIST ROLES

Because they desire to move from problem to problem and skill to skill, they tend to thrive in roles where they have the opportunity to utilize a wide range of aptitudes. They might work on a website in the morning, lead a sales meeting in the afternoon, and develop a product strategy before calling it quits for the day. They are not likely to be the absolute best at any of these functions, but they may be skilled enough to do an acceptable job.

ORGANIZATIONS THAT SERVE VARIOUS NEEDS

The most important thing for a person driven to Demonstrate New Learning is that the work doesn't become redundant. Therefore, they are well suited for consultancies or creative agency work that allows them to apply many different skills throughout the week.

JOBS WHERE THEY CAN SIMPLIFY COMPLEX TOPICS

People motivated to Demonstrate New Learning are very good at taking big, complex issues and simplifying them for others. So they often prefer roles that allow them to teach others a new process or skill that they themselves have learned. However, watch that they don't force simplicity where it isn't warranted, or fail to recognize nuances in a subject or skill.

15: EXPLORE

You are driven to explore what is unknown and perhaps mysterious to you, pressing beyond the existing limits of your knowledge and/or experience.

Jill uses all her vacation days. Twice a year, she visits a new city where she doesn't know a single person and spends the days strolling through parks, exploring bookstores, and wandering into neighborhood restaurants. Her travels take her all over the world, even to places where she doesn't speak the language. She loves immersing herself in new cultures and learning how to communicate as she goes. When she returns home, she always shares her adventures with friends and coworkers, many of whom think she's a little odd for jumping into these adventures with both feet. But Jill couldn't imagine living any other way.

Crazy about Novel Experiences

Like Jill, some people are always on the go, trying new experiences, eating at different restaurants, learning exotic hobbies, or taking vacations to less-traveled destinations. They have many stories about exciting experiences they've had or plan to have. At work, they are the ones driving the exploratory process and pushing the team to venture into uncomfortable territory when determining a strategy or generating ideas for a project. They crave novel approaches—if it's been done before, they're not interested.

Willing to Push the Limit

Those motivated to Explore are driven to go beyond the limits of their knowledge to discover what's unknown. They tend to be very curious and seek adventure, sometimes skewing toward the adrenaline-junkie end of the spectrum. The novelty of the experience is what primarily motivates them. They want to experience rare things or discover new techniques. This doesn't mean they have to travel to do so; they are adept at finding opportunities around them that provide the unique experiences they crave. In fact, they could spend weeks in their own city discovering all it has to offer.

They don't pass judgment, but are willing to entertain ideas that others might balk at. They grow bored with the status quo or projects that don't let them venture out to the edges of their capabilities. Therefore, as in all areas of their life, they want to do work that stimulates them and provides novel experiences.

Idea Generators

Most of the time, they have more ideas than they know what to do with. As a result, they thrive in the early, exploratory stages of a project, such as brainstorming and setting strategy, but sometimes tend to struggle as the project moves into the execution phase. Predictability is their primary foe, and they will do whatever it takes to keep their options open.

Inspirational

Those motivated to Explore inspire others with their unique stories and ideas. Because of their wide range of insights in a lot of areas, they are able to formulate ideas that others may not have seen before. As a result, they often push the team into new and uncomfortable territory, or to pursue unexpected avenues of exploration that can lead to valuable innovations.

The Shadow Side

Along with all their positive qualities, there are a handful of areas where those motivated to Explore can slip into unhealthy behavior:

THEY OFTEN FAIL TO FOLLOW THROUGH

Because they are motivated to find new ways of doing things or to develop new skills, they might struggle to stay the course and see things through to the end. When they are distracted with new possibilities, they are prone to follow those exciting new threads instead of sticking with the plan.

THEY CAN IGNORE THE RULES

If they feel your expectations or parameters are too limiting, they might ignore them to chase after an idea. They dislike administrative work or anything that seems too repetitive, like staff meetings or recurring tasks often necessary to the work of the team. If they don't believe a rule should apply to them, or if it feels too confining, they might simply ignore it without telling you. Others on the team more likely to abide by expectations might feel such behavior is a lapse in team culture and lose trust in the team and its leadership.

THEY PUSH BOUNDARIES, EVEN WHEN IT'S UNCALLED FOR

At times, they might challenge the rules or explore beyond the bounds of the predetermined scope of a project, even when told not to do so. They are often the ones to challenge the status quo. If their role isn't satisfying their need to explore, they will take it upon themselves to redefine their duties in a way that gives them the latitude to satisfy their need for novelty, even if it's not officially ordained by the organization.

THEY CAN BECOME DISSATISFIED WITH DAILY ROUTINES

Explore-motivated individuals often desire change just for the sake of change. If they lead a team, they might be perpetually tinkering with the group's systems, policies, and expectations. When they begin to feel stifled, they might blow things up and start over, which can create a lack of stability among team members. To them, every day would ideally feel like an adventure.

Working with an Explore Person

SET WIDE BOUNDARIES

They will not respond well to overly constrictive or controlling processes and expectations. Instead, establish a playing field and let them have some degree of freedom in how they approach the project. If you tell them what to do, they might respond by inappropriately challenging your directives, but if you give them options for how to handle the problem, they will reward you with innovative thought and personal engagement. Be willing to modify your plans if their efforts take the project in a direction you did not expect. Now, this isn't always possible. There will be times you'll need to be more directive due to time pressure or organizational expectations. In these situations, have a frank conversation with them about why this situation is unique, and remind them that it's temporal and there will be opportunities to explore around the next turn.

DEFINE GOING DEEPER AS A FORM OF EXPLORATION

Because they are often easily distracted, they can leave a wake of half-finished projects. Challenge them to dive deeper into their work, or a particular project, as a way to satisfy their exploration drive. Ask them specific questions to guide their investigation, such as "What if we...?"

or "Have you considered . . . ?" Novelty can be uncovered even in familiar work if you help them frame it up properly.

PRIORITIZE THE EARLY STAGES OF THE PROJECT

They will not be driven to complete a project. Instead, they will perform better in the early, open-ended phases where there is more opportunity to explore. Find ways to utilize them in this early stage, and give them wide latitude to get a head start on the rest of the team, especially in any kind of work the group hasn't engaged in before. Provide the Explore-motivated individual the space and resources they need to find new stimuli to fuel the team's process.

KEEP DEVELOPMENT PLANS OPEN-ENDED

Sometimes you might feel the need to be very directive and concrete with them in terms of their personal development. However, your relationship with the person motivated to Explore will be more of a dance than a march. Understand that your role is to help them discover the path they should be traveling, not to tell them what it is. So you must learn to be a good coach, ask great questions, and prepare for flexibility. Know that they bring diversity of thought and experience to the table that cannot be matched by those motivated in other ways, and that they are often the ones keeping the team on its toes. Strive to see this as a positive thing, even when you grow frustrated with their distractibility.

Where They Thrive

CREATIVE INDUSTRIES

Those driven to Explore ask more questions than the team is usually comfortable with, but that means they are challenging the team to think in new ways that often yield brilliant, non-intuitive ideas. Because of this, they tend to thrive in roles that allow them to explore, challenge assumptions, and venture into less-trafficked areas of thought.

RESEARCH AND DEVELOPMENT

Because they are often tinkerers by nature, they're often driven to be on the cutting edge, especially if there's potential for a big payoff if successful. They love to question assumptions and challenge conventional wisdom, often to the chagrin of those around them. Thus, they are motivated to find the needle-in-a-haystack idea others think is impossible.

ROLES THAT OFFER NEW EXPERIENCES

Maybe they frequently get to travel to new locations, or they get to work with exotic and interesting people, or they get to dive into brand-new subjects or markets consistently. Regardless, people driven to Explore will be most gratified with the work they are doing when they are operating beyond their comfort zone.

THE LEARNER FAMILY: CONCLUSION

Those whose Motivation Code is made up of themes within the Learner Family are out on the fringes exploring possibility and keeping the rest of the team thinking about what's next. When they are attached to the right projects, they have the potential to expand your team's thinking in unexpected ways.

If you are motivated by one of these themes, here are a few tips for structuring your life and work for maximum effectiveness:

Recognize That Not Everyone Is Wired Like You

Know that your motivation to explore, ask questions, and venture out into new territory might (from time to time) rub people the wrong way. It's not that they dislike you or your motivation—it's that they simply derive their energy in different ways. When you experience this tension, see it as an opportunity to explain the motivation driving your behavior and ask how you can be of help. Remember there are times to explore and learn and master, and there are times to check tasks off lists.

Develop a Side Project or Hobby

There will be times when work will not allow you the latitude for exploring and learning. If that's the case, it's important you have some other outlet for these motivations so you don't go off course in your work. Find a hobby, a topic to explore, or a side project that allows you to satisfy your urge to learn. Your work is a portfolio of activities that includes, but is not completely comprised of, your full-time job, so make sure you have a diverse range of activities in your life to help you stay engaged.

Make a Bucket List

Write down a list of recommended books on topics you're interested in. Make a list of places you'd like to go before you die. Think about the skills you'd like to learn this year and the resources that can help you accomplish them. Plan your learning so you have something to look forward to.

Consider the Application

Because you'll be absorbing stimuli nearly constantly, train yourself to consider questions like "How does this apply to the project we're working on?" or "How might this apply to the big meeting we have on Tuesday?" By directing your learning toward concrete, time-sensitive work activities, you will find that you're in a better position to leverage your natural motivations and aptitudes toward ends the team finds helpful as well.

Chapter Seven

THE OPTIMIZER FAMILY

Common Characteristics

- Derives their energy from making things efficient
- Wants systems and information to be organized
- Focused on getting it right from the beginning rather than fixing it later
- Needs to lay firm foundations for future work, and isn't concerned about being "known" for their contribution

THOSE MOTIVATED BY THE OPTIMIZER FAMILY THEMES ARE OFTEN THE people most likely to start organizing their desk while they meet with you. But they're also the person you want in charge of your organization's operations, as they are able to squeeze the most value possible out of a system, and to ensure there is nothing wasted. They also tend to gravitate toward fixing problems others have come to accept. They can rarely pass by something that's not functioning properly without making an attempt to right the wrong. As such, they can be a valuable right-hand person to a Visionary CEO or leader, because they are able to spot the inherent flaws in the details of the big picture.

Those driven by the Optimizer Family themes are motivated to set up an operation on firm foundations and/or ensure that systems function well. They come alive when they are extracting the most potential out of a system (or person).

There are six motivational themes that fall within the Optimizer Family:

1. Organize
2. Make It Right
3. Improve
4. Make It Work
5. Develop
6. Establish

16: ORGANIZE

You want to set up and maintain a smooth-running operation.

A lot of people have ideas for how the world could be better, but Tracy couldn't rest unless she acted on hers. Whether it was a bake sale fundraiser for the local elementary school or a group of citizens expressing concern at a city council meeting, Tracy was always right in the middle, pulling it together. She loved to corral people toward a common cause, and felt deeply gratified when engaged in organizing communications, tasks, and gatherings. At work, she would always arrive at a meeting having thought through the critical path to accomplishing the team's next objective. So much so that the team often overly depended on her to streamline the workflow and was lost without her. Tracy, as you may have guessed, is motivated to Organize.

Repulsed by Chaos

The theme of Organize is not just about the ability to organize, which many people have, but the deep drive to do so. Organize-motivated individuals can't stand for things to be in chaos. They enjoy the sense of potential involved in putting all the pieces together and making them work collectively.

Detail Oriented

They also tend to be very detailed, and often want to be deeply involved in controlling all aspects of a project or situation. They don't do well when they must cede control to others, especially when they don't trust the organizational skills of the other person. As a result, even when they delegate, they often closely monitor progress to ensure that everything is going according to plan.

Those motivated to Organize often have a great range of skills, both hard and soft. They are able to structure complex projects and teams well, plan even in the face of uncertainty, influence others to follow the plans they've mapped, and manage their team toward objectives. They have earned the trust of others due to their attention to detail. They are often motivated to stick with projects or initiatives over a long period of time, and seem to rarely get bored with their responsibilities.

Excellent Entrepreneurs

Many people driven to Organize are highly successful in entrepreneurial roles because they are able to break big problems into manageable chunks to tackle one at a time. They see the trees as well as the forest.

The Shadow Side

Personally, I'm deeply grateful for those driven to Organize because having them around often helps make things much more functional. However, there are also some shadow-side attributes to be mindful of:

THEY SHUT DOWN IN SOLO ROLES

If there is no one to organize, or the project work is too simple, they might shut down or be less motivated to complete the work. So much of their motivation is about bringing clarity and sanity to complex situations, and if the work or relationships become too predictable, they are likely to disengage.

THEY CAN OVEREXTEND THEMSELVES

Because they are often control minded, they tend to get involved in the nitty-gritty of the work. But they also want to keep track of each phase of an operation and how they fit together. This practice of maintaining big- and small-picture activity can lead to burnout.

THEY TEND TO CONTROL

They can sometimes be guilty of bottlenecking the team's work, because they have to be involved in every decision and approve every direction the team takes on a project. Highly talented, creative people on their team might be turned off by this excessive need for control and could begin looking for other opportunities. It's important to the person motivated to Organize that their vision be central to the work, and if they aren't directly involved they begin to worry that the project is in danger of drifting off the rails. They can often be a bit pushy and dogmatic. They decided that the tradeoff for some of their many gifts is that they struggle with excessive precision and might at times run their work, their personal life, and their family like a military operation, demanding the highest level of performance and coordination.

*THEY GET RESTLESS IN THE ABSENCE
OF BIG ORGANIZATIONAL CHALLENGES*

If there aren't any big projects or uncertainties for them to wrangle, they can grow antsy and even seek to insert themselves where they don't belong just to have something to do. They need to feel they are constantly organizing, adding value, and pushing things forward.

Working with an Organize Person

GIVE THEM WORK THAT REQUIRES ORGANIZATION

It might sound obvious, but they thrive on bringing order in the midst of chaos, and in optimizing things that have fallen into disrepair, such as a process that has been patched together over the years and needs rethinking, or a reporting structure that has grown too convoluted and confusing to the team. Unlike with many of the other themes, those driven to Organize are drawn to situations where they can insert themselves and bring efficiency. Make certain you aren't assigning them too much repetitive, predictable work, but are instead allowing them the freedom to use their motivation to further the organization's objectives.

STAY ATTUNED TO THEIR TENDENCY TO OVERWORK

It's very important that you, if you are their manager, probe regularly to identify any areas where they might be overextending themselves or trying to tackle more than they have the resources to accomplish. If you notice they seem to be threadbare and irritable, ask them about their workload and see if you can spot where they are (a) trying to control too much to the point that it's overwhelming them, or (b) attempting to organize work that is simply too unmanageable to tackle at this time.

> **Signs an Organize Person Is Stretched Too Thin**
>
> - They have a short fuse or get irrationally angry over small areas of disorganization.
> - They turn molehills into mountains, stressing over what no one else is even thinking about.
> - They let their own personal organization slip to meet the organizational needs of the team.
> - They try to exert excessive control over areas where they have no authority so they can get ahead of the work.

GIVE THEM GROUP WORK

Make certain their work is balanced with collaborative or leadership efforts, or projects. If left to solo work for too long, they might begin to insert themselves into places they don't belong. Give them permission to invite others into a project. Allow them the freedom to build their own team, or to invite others into the work as they see fit. If they are handed a team that's already established and has clear processes and protocols, they might not respond with a full measure of enthusiasm, nor will their gifts be best utilized. Encourage them to bring their own organizational perspective to projects.

GRANT THEM FLEXIBILITY IN HOW THEY APPROACH THEIR WORK

Don't prescribe processes to them. Instead, let them bring order to the work in the way they think best. Those motivated to Organize are engaged as much with the process of the work as with the end results, so don't squelch that enthusiasm by being overly controlling. However, stay closely connected to their decisions and demand accountability for how they are using organizational resources. Make certain they aren't being overly controlling themselves, but are allowing team members to bring their full motivation and skill set to the table each day.

ENCOURAGE THEM TO INVOLVE OTHERS IN THE WORK

At times, those motivated to Organize can slip into seeing people only as a means to an end. When this happens, they might disconnect from the emotional and energy needs of the team and think only about time and efficiency and getting things done. For example, they might assign tasks to people who are obviously already overloaded, or grow angry with someone for having a good idea because it might push the project beyond its expected timeline.

Make sure they have a good grasp on the temperament of their team members and are paying attention to the team's needs beyond the requirements of the work.

Where They Thrive

OPERATIONS

Because they have the innate drive to put everything in its proper place, Organize-motivated individuals are often able to join a team and quickly assess what's broken and how to fix it. They are driven to solve problems and help systems run as efficiently as possible, so it's important they have both the permission and resources necessary to bring order to whatever is in disarray. If they do, they will be your chief problem solver and hole plugger. They are also likely to thrive in roles that involve designing or planning spaces, but that also need attention to detail, like interior design or engineering.

MANAGEMENT

They can see all the pieces, both the forest and the trees, and understand how to work them together to accomplish objectives. They perform well as project managers or managers of teams with defined outcomes and resources to be managed. They will ensure that all the right parts are in place to help the team succeed, and will put everyone in the suitable role so the team is functioning properly. City planning and project management are examples of positions requiring the Organize-motivated person's problem-solving and organizational skills.

PROCESS-ORIENTED WORK

They derive energy from management of a well-organized process. They will work hard to make the process as efficient as possible, or to guide a long-arc project to its ultimate end, making whatever tweaks are necessary along the way to keep it on course.

17: MAKE IT RIGHT

You consistently set up or follow standards, procedures, and principles that you believe are right.

On December 1, 1955, Rosa Parks refused to give up her seat to a white person on a Montgomery, Alabama, bus. Although she was not the first African American to protest the unjust segregation laws prevalent in the southern United States in the 1950s, her bold action and willingness to hold firm for what she believed in sparked massive bus boycotts and other forms of social protest throughout the South, eventually snowballing into the civil rights movement and subsequent legislation outlawing segregation. When later asked how she summoned the courage in the face of backlash and violence, she said, "You must never be fearful about what you are doing when it is right."

While few people will be called on to take such a brave, prominent stance at great danger to themselves and their loved ones, all people motivated to Make It Right are driven by a need to abide by what they believe to be right, just, and fair.

Devoted to Clear Standards

Those motivated to Make It Right want to consistently follow ideals and principles they bring to all their efforts and involvements. They have clear standards for their work, and it's important to them that they and their teammates abide by those standards and do things the "right way." Even successful work that's done improperly might feel like a failure to them. To be satisfied with the results, they must believe that everything was done correctly. They have a drive for precision and a desire for clarity. Their mortal enemy is vagueness, whether in expectations or process.

Strong Moral Compass

They are not afraid to defend what they believe is right, in spite of opposition. They will take a minority position and stand against the tide to do what they perceive to be right and proper. While this sometimes causes tension with others, they are also typically admired for their principled approach to life and work, and inspire others around them by their example. They are exemplars of integrity, and expect professionalism and forthrightness from their colleagues. They are often the standard-bearer for the organization, whether or not it's their "official" responsibility.

Unafraid to Speak Up

They are not afraid to speak up or voice their position on an issue, even when others fear the consequences of doing so. They are outspoken about new projects, ideas, or organizational changes, offering their thoughts on how they line up with the core values of the organization.

The Shadow Side

While their desire to Make It Right often provides a clear moral compass for themselves and their team, there are a few shadow-side attributes to watch out for:

THEY CAN EXPERIENCE EXTREME STRESS
IF WORK DOESN'T REFLECT VALUES

When their personal values conflict with those of the organization, it can create a high degree of stress both for the team and for them personally. They might struggle to reconcile their desire to do things the right way with organizational expectations that don't align with their personal values. This is also true when, as a manager of a team, their values don't align with those of the people they are tasked with leading. The dissonance can create tension in the relationship, and they can be guilty of trying to conform the team member to their standards and expectations rather than allowing them the freedom to bring their own motivation and values to the work.

THEY CAN SEE THE WORLD IN BLACK AND WHITE

Because of their high standards, they often miss the nuance and value of other people's perspective. In order to hold fast to their own expectations, they often parse the world into black and white, good and bad, acceptable and unacceptable, and are unwilling to compromise or see any common ground between themselves and others.

THEY ARE CRITICAL OF THEMSELVES AND OTHERS

Because of their high standards, they can be difficult to be around for an extended period of time. They tend to be on the lookout for ways in which things aren't what they should be, and aren't afraid of levying critiques at others when those standards aren't met. They are especially

How Make It Right Sees It	How Everyone Else Sees It
This is clearly an outrage!	I can kind of see both sides...
This is the worst work I've ever seen.	I think this could be good with a few tweaks.
I have failed miserably.	I was 10 percent short of my goal, but still did pretty well. I'll hit it next time.
This is the most important thing I've ever worked on.	This is a pretty important project.

hard on themselves, and might find it difficult to celebrate good work because they never feel like it was good enough.

THEY TRY TO LIVE UP TO IMPOSSIBLY HIGH STANDARDS

They are often guilty of setting the bar far too high, or expecting a kind of perfection that's simply unrealistic. They might drive their team to exhaustion in their attempt to get it right. And those standards by which they measure the work are often far above and beyond what the organization or client would expect. As such, it's possible for them to cause tension on a team when their motivation to do things the right way interferes with someone else's motivation to simply get things done. They might find their strict adherence to certain protocols or principles runs against some of the inclinations of the more efficiency-minded team members, so the Make It Right person can feel to everyone else on the team like a bottleneck in the system.

THEY CAN BE CLOSED-MINDED

The Make It Right person's view of the world is often set, and they see it as the responsibility of others to conform to their vision rather than finding appropriate middle ground themselves. As a result, they often find negotiation challenging because they cannot compromise. Instead, they will walk away from a potentially valuable deal if they don't believe the other party is willing to live up to their personal standards and expectations. For example, while a potential business partnership might make financial sense on paper, if they perceive that the other party is sloppy in email communications, or that their hiring standards are too soft, they might pass on the deal.

Working with a Make It Right Person

BE CLEAR AND PRECISE

Your expectations and all communication with them must be precise, and must align with organizational policies and protocol. Vagueness is your enemy, because it will cause them to disconnect from whatever you're telling them, no matter how important it might be. Take the time necessary to collect your thoughts, and be prepared for your conversation with them. Don't try to wing it.

HELP THEM DEFINE THEIR BATTLES

Those driven to Make It Right can be tempted to fight every battle, every time, but that's simply not realistic. They must choose which battles are most important and which to forget about to deliver on their objectives. If you are their manager, you must help them understand which principles they should fight for and which might be less important given the work on their plate. Don't allow them to become worn or burned out because they are trying to slay multiple dragons at once.

POINT OUT WHERE THEY MIGHT BE GOING OVERBOARD WITH EXPECTATIONS

They might not see the places in their life where they are being too rigid, or where they are layering too much onto those around them. If you are their manager, help them identify the areas where they are creating undue stress on the organization, or where their standards are simply unrealistically high. Examples might include requiring team members to follow very strict processes rather than allowing them to complete the work however it seems best, or expecting a policy they disagree with to disappear overnight rather than being satisfied with its more realistic, gradual removal.

ENCOURAGE EMPATHY

By asking them leading questions, you can help them better understand how their approach is affecting their team. For example, questions like "How do you think Jill felt when you critiqued her work in front of the team?" or "How do you think the team feels about your timeline for this project?" can be helpful to jump into a conversation about the team's needs. You might have to actively help them imagine these feelings and scenarios, as they might not naturally do so without your prompting.

HELP THEM SET RELATIONAL GOALS

Because they are often focused on quantitative measurement, like ratios and goal targets, those motivated to Make It Right might struggle to determine how a relationship is going. Relationships are, by nature, qualitative and difficult to measure. Help them understand how to read relational cues such as quality of conversations, positive interactions, and a sense of connection to determine the state of their work relationships.

Where They Thrive

STANDARD-BEARER ROLES

They are motivated to align their activities and those of the people they lead with the values of the organization, therefore any role that allows them to champion organizational standards will resonate with them. Leading big cultural initiatives within the company or being tasked with bringing the entire organization into alignment with new policies will be work they enjoy and excel at. Additionally, they tend to be effective at leading the charge on righting a great wrong or solving an injustice. They cannot rest until it is rectified.

PROCESS WORK THAT IS REPEATABLE

They will pursue perfection not only in outcome, but in execution. As such, work that allows them to refine their skills and perfect their performance will be gratifying. On the other hand, work that requires a different approach each time, or where the desired results vary from case to case, might cause anxiety as they strive to figure out what "right" means in each situation.

Even though the word "bureaucrat" often takes on a negative meaning, those who strive to Make It Right often thrive in roles where there are clear guidelines for how to accomplish something, and they will become a fierce defender of the process, which ensures that everything gets done properly.

ROLES WITH A CLEAR CHAIN OF COMMAND

They flourish under clear leadership and effective commands. For example, many who are motivated to Make It Right come alive in a military environment, where the principles of behavior are crystal clear and the commands are unequivocal. They know exactly how to do things the proper way, and they understand the consequences for getting it wrong. Additionally, there is often a very black-and-white view of the world, with little room to argue or negotiate. Vagueness can be lethal.

18: IMPROVE

You are happiest when you are using your abilities to make things better.

It was never good enough for Kevin. Regardless of what his team did, he always seemed to find some fault or some way their work could be better. The day before a pitch to an important client, he would ask to see multiple versions with different fonts. He would critique and second-guess their strategy, right up until the pitch was delivered, making everyone around him nervous just when they needed to be most confident. Over time, the team learned to accept the fact that he was a perfectionist and would never be satisfied. The odd thing is, all of this was news to Kevin. He never thought his feedback was unreasonable. After all, most of the tweaks were minor, and as far as he could tell, they all made the project much better. He was uncertain why his team was so frustrated with him.

Kevin was simply following his motivation to Improve. He's driven to find ways that things can be better, even when others think things are fine as they are. This resulted in successful work but strained relationships. Once he learned how his motivation was affecting those around him, he was able to frame his feedback in a way that felt less perfectionistic, and more motivational to the team as well.

Things Can Always Be Better

Those driven to Improve are consistently seeking to make things better, or to enhance them in some way. They can easily see the ways something could be optimized or tweaked to make it more effective, palatable, or engaging. They scan their surroundings nearly constantly in search of something to improve. They find ways of enriching a situation long after others have moved on to new projects or have deemed it perfect. They enjoy playing with new configurations, testing and refining the efficiency of a system or organization.

Tim loved to frequent a local coffee shop, just down the road from his home, on the way to work. It was one of those noncorporate businesses, and was definitely very laid-back in both its atmosphere and operations. Tim loved the coffee, but sometimes the way the coffee shop was run would grate on his nerves.

One particular struggle that Tim had was the way the service line was set up. Customers would pay for their coffee at the cash register, then serve themselves. The first problem was that the coffee cups and sleeves were on the opposite end of the service line from where you paid. As such, you would pay for the coffee, then walk to the other end, past cisterns of coffee, to get your cup. Then you would walk down the line to choose your coffee.

And that's when you'd encounter problem number two: the cream and sugar were back at the front of the line, where you picked up your coffee cup. So Tim would pour his coffee, then fight back through the line of customers to the cream-and-sugar table, where he could make his coffee the way he pleased.

For most customers, this was a minor nuisance they probably didn't think twice about. However, Tim's motivation is Improve. Multiple times he attempted to move cups to the other end of the line, or move the cream and sugar to a location that made more sense, but the next day he would come back and they would be in their former nonsensical positions. He even tried to talk to the employees, to no avail. Finally, Tim decided to give up on the local joint and hit the Starbucks a few blocks up the street instead. Yes, it was corporate, but it was convenient and the systems didn't drive him crazy.

While this is an extreme example, it is not at all uncommon for those motivated to Improve. They are driven to make things operate efficiently and with purpose. When they encounter something that is out of sorts, or that could be better, they are drawn to fix it and help it function at its best.

At their heart, they want to leave things better than how they found them. This is how they know their work matters, and that they are making a difference in the lives of people they encounter. They tend to be generalists by nature, and are able to find efficiencies or improvements even in areas that aren't within their core expertise.

Able to Add Value

They are often recognized for producing more value from existing assets, relationships, systems, clients, or products. (They are the ones who squeeze that last little bit of toothpaste out of the tube before tossing it in the garbage!) Somehow, they always seem able to stretch existing resources further and with more impact than others around them.

Everything Has Potential

They also tend to see the potential in things. They are miners of diamonds in the rough. They recognize areas where people or resources are being underutilized and figure out how to draw out their maximum potential. Because of this, they tend to be good managers; they won't allow others to settle for good enough. Instead, they are obsessed with helping those around them improve and produce more value than they believe they are capable of.

The Shadow Side

As with all motivations, there are some shadow-side watch points for those motivated to Improve. Many of them center around their tendency to get involved when they aren't necessarily welcome, or to struggle to gain improvement out of people or systems simply uninterested in change. Here are some:

STEPPING ON TOES AND OFFERING UNWANTED SUGGESTIONS OR ADVICE

Because they see opportunity for improvement everywhere, they can sometimes be guilty of meddling in the lives and work of others, and can offer unwanted suggestions for improvement. They might say, "You know, this could be better if you . . ." or "Have you considered . . . ?" even when you didn't ask for—or want—their opinion. As you can imagine, this can cause tension on the team, especially if others feel their work is constantly under the judging eyes of the person driven to Improve. It's important for Improve individuals to understand which situations lend themselves to offering suggestions and which are best left alone.

CAN BECOME PARALYZED WITH "WHITE SPACE" OR A "BLANK SHEET"

While they are excessively gifted and motivated to improve existing systems and ideas, they often struggle to generate ideas out of nowhere. Thus, they can be of limited help at the beginning of a project or when the team is exploring new territory. They need to have some guardrails to help them direct their work in the right way.

THEY CAN BE EXCESSIVELY HARD ON THEMSELVES AND OTHERS, EVEN IN SUCCESS

Because of their drive for constant improvement, it can feel like they are riding others all the time and are never satisfied with their output. They make frequent suggestions for optimization, even in the wake of a huge victory or celebration. This can leave others feeling deflated and judged.

THEY STRUGGLE TO ACCEPT WHAT CANNOT BE CHANGED

They have a difficult time with situations beyond help, or with others who simply do not want to improve. They struggle to relate to people or organizations happy with the status quo, and they might stretch too far to adapt behavior to make it optimal. Again, this can create tension on the team as the Improve-motivated individual strikes the same note over and over, despite the fact that no one seems to listen or care.

Working with an Improve Person

HELP THEM DECIPHER WHAT CAN AND CAN'T BE CHANGED

Offer your perspective on situations where you believe they are trying to accomplish something that is simply unfeasible. If they are struggling to extract the final percentage of improvement from a project at great expense of time and energy to the organization, help them see that those resources could be better spent in other areas. Routinely discuss with them their priorities and where they plan to spend their time and focus in the coming days, and be on the lookout for ways they might be overdoing it in any specific area.

One way to identify this is to ask, "Is there any area of responsibility right now that you just can't seem to get *right*?" or "What's the most frustrating part of your job at the moment?" Either of these questions are likely to yield insight into where they are spending too much energy improving projects or processes that are already good enough.

ASSIGN THEM TO PROJECTS THAT REQUIRE CONSTANT OPTIMIZATION

Rather than putting the Improve-motivated individual in situations where the work is fast and uncertain, allow them to own some work requiring them to spend significant time identifying and leveraging efficiencies. These could be redesigning systems, reorganizing teams, or working to improve communication processes within the organization. However, make certain you keep a close eye on *how* they are going about this work, so that they aren't exasperating their coworkers. Give them a clear metric by which they will know they've crossed the finish line and can move on to other projects. This is especially important, because otherwise they will be motivated to keep tweaking and improving until they run out of time or resources.

HELP THEM UNDERSTAND THE BIG PICTURE

Those motivated to Improve often get lost in the details of the work, and the net result is that they can't see the results of their work in a macro sense. Instead, they focus on how everything would be better if the work was only a little more ideal. Talk with them about specific ways their work is creating value, and help them see that imperfect work done well can have more net impact than perfect work that is never finished.

OFFER THEM SPECIFIC SUGGESTIONS FOR IMPROVEMENT

They are motivated to Improve, so give them specific and concrete ways you believe they could do their work better. They will thrive on this kind of feedback. (On the flip side, don't offer them vague and platitude-laden advice or feedback. It will be unhelpful.) For each one-on-one, offer suggestions for how you think they could improve their leadership, their collaboration with others, or the work they are doing for the organization. Make sure your suggestions are reasonable and actionable. The Improve-driven person will receive this feedback as encouragement, not critique.

Where They Thrive

PROJECT OR ORGANIZATIONAL DEVELOPMENT ROLES

Improve-motivated individuals are driven to take something from just okay to excellent. They perform well in roles where they are given freedom to tweak, experiment with, and change a process or product. They will also do well with projects needing constant attention or continual improvement, such as coding new software or mixing an audio recording until it's just right. Conversely, they don't do well with blank sheets and no parameters, like inventing a new product or hiring and leading a brand-new team. They need to have something to work with so they can identify the diamond in the rough.

PEOPLE DEVELOPMENT ROLES

Similarly, they are excellent at helping others excel. They are able to spot areas of potential improvement in others and can help them optimize their performance. They often make excellent coaches, teachers, or consultants because they are able to spot potential opportunities for others even in an area outside their core competency. They will replay scenarios in their head after a meeting or interaction and think of how to do things better next time, often offering that advice to those around them. (This is sometimes true even when the advice isn't asked for or wanted!)

ROLES WHERE SUCCESS IS EASILY MEASURED

They are motivated to build upon past success and continuously move toward excellence, so any work that allows them the opportunity to know the "score" will energize them. For example, sales roles with concrete targets or shepherding a product line with a specified goal for market share growth are ideal. Work where the standards of success are vague or where "good enough" is the target will quickly lose their interest. They need to know what the score is and know how to top it tomorrow.

19: MAKE IT WORK

Your motivation focuses on fixing something that has broken down or is functioning poorly.

The 1940s ushered in the very beginning of the computer age as military and civilian organizations began experimenting with machines that could perform complex computations in a fraction of the time it would take humans. One of those early computing pioneers was Grace Hopper. She was a professor of mathematics at Vassar College, but in 1943 she enlisted in the United States Navy to help with the war effort, working on several critical computing projects and transforming computer science. She was critical in inventing computer languages, and stories of her contribution to the field of computer science are legendary. In one instance, she pulled a moth that was causing issues from a computer, saying she had "debugged" the machine, coining a phrase that's still used today to talk about fixing problems with computer code.

Hopper was known as a quintessential problem solver. Her colleagues said they would end the workday by discussing a problem, and when they arrived the next morning, Grace had a solution. In reflecting on her career, she once said, "I have always been fascinated with how things work and making things work." This sentiment could be the mantra of the person motivated to Make It Work.

Natural Fixers

Those motivated to Make It Work are driven to fix something that has broken down or is functioning poorly. They are fascinated by governing dynamics and the potential of the object, operation, or people with whom they are working. They tend to exhibit a high degree of grit when it comes to tackling difficult challenges, and are hesitant to give up until the job is complete.

Practical Minded

They tend to be very practical and thorough, always seeking solutions that can be executed in the near term rather than focusing on theory or longer-term objectives.

They are talented at dissecting nuance and getting to the root of the matter; they can identify the single cause in a nest of causes that is truly the heart of a problem. They bring wonderful analytical and investigative skills and are able to simplify complex matters for those who need to better understand them.

Quick to Move On

Unlike some of the other Optimizer motivational themes, they are less focused on routine maintenance and more focused on concrete troubleshooting activities. They want to identify and fix a problem, then move on. They are not likely to linger once they feel they've fulfilled their responsibility to a project or situation, but will instead move on to the next problem to solve.

They tend to be very effective at quickly diagnosing problems and getting a project, system, or organization back on track. They are the turnaround specialists brought in to right a leaning ship. However, they quickly grow weary once the core problem has been solved and tend to want to move on to the next challenge.

Creative

Finally, they tend to be creative problem solvers, and can generate many possible solutions to a tough situation. Their resourcefulness allows them to draw from a number of previous issues they've solved or have been a part of solving and apply that learning to the current situation.

The Shadow Side

Their problem-solving abilities make the Make It Work person a useful and resourceful asset. However, there are also a few shadow side attributes to be mindful of.

THEY SEE PROBLEMS EVERYWHERE

They are often prone to making mountains out of molehills. Because they are wired to identify and solve problems, they will sometimes see them even where they don't exist. For instance, in the middle of doing a client project, they might identify a problem with the project management tool that the team is using, and spend precious time trying to fix that process instead of focusing on the actual objectives. When they raise issues or preemptively jump in to fix something that no one else even thinks is broken, it can cause unnecessary distraction in their workgroup. These needless delays and diversions in the course of the work can take a toll, especially if they are tasked with leading others.

THEY TINKER WITHOUT COUNTING THE COST TO OTHERS

They might blow up a system or tinker with a process because they want to better understand how it works. However, this can have a negative effect on those still trying to function in the midst of their tinkering. Those motivated to Make It Work are often oblivious to the effects of their actions. They are simply following their curiosity where it leads.

THEY CAN CREATE INSTABILITY

Because they struggle with letting things be good enough, they might shift systems, expectations, and other workplace norms constantly. Their attempts to set things right can have a cost to the organization's efficiency and ability to actually do the work. Others who are more motivated for progress might find their constant tinkering intolerable.

THEY NEED FRESH CHALLENGES

If they are in a role requiring constant, ongoing service of a system or client but with minimal problems to be solved, they will grow discontent and can begin looking for problems where they don't exist. They might even create problems—break things—just to fix them. They are fixers by nature, and they get restless without a problem to tackle.

They might also become discontent and turned off by smooth-running operations that don't require their problem-solving skills. If there isn't an intervention needed, they simply aren't interested.

Working with a Make It Work Person

The key to helping them bring their best effort is in focusing their problem-solving prowess on the right issues at the right time. As a manager, you must stay in constant conversation with them about problems they're working on and progress they're making on important initiatives.

ASSIGN THEM TO PROBLEMS, NOT OPEN-ENDED PROJECTS OR PROCESSES

This is a big one. They don't function well long-term inside of a well-oiled machine. They will grow bored and frustrated, and might start breaking things just so they have something to fix. They are your go-to fixers when something is broken or not operating as it should, so leverage that motivation to its fullest! Allow them to bring their resourcefulness to bear against the organization's toughest sticking points.

FOCUS ON THE PRACTICAL IMPLICATIONS OF DECISIONS AND IDEAS

They don't always function well in the realm of the theoretical. You must help them see the real-world application of decisions you're making or ideas you're introducing. What does this solve? How does it apply directly to the work we're doing? What does this fix? You can't rely on them to connect the dots, but must instead help them see how your actions assist them in making concrete progress on problems they are solving.

ALLOW THEM TO EXPERIENCE SOME SHORT-TERM, EASY WINS

Make certain their portfolio of work includes at least some projects that allow for easy, short-term victories. They need to feel they are making measurable progress in solving problems, and if their workload is all long-term horizons they will grow listless. Give them a few short-term projects, like planning a meeting or reorganizing a scheduling system, even if it means taking some of their time and energy away from important longer-term organizational initiatives. They will reward you with better work on the more important projects.

TREAT RELATIONAL ISSUES LIKE PROBLEMS TO BE SOLVED

Because they are tinkerers by nature, they are not inclined to solve less concrete emotional or relational problems without first pulling apart the dynamics of the relationship to figure out what's broken. Some are more analytical than intuitive by nature, so they will be most comfortable approaching relational issues in an engineered way. Go with them on this problem-solving quest and talk them through the issues in a concise, measured way. For example, ask questions like "What is the root cause of your tension with Bill?" or "What could you do differently in your one-on-ones with Sarah to make them more effective?" Ask specific, concrete questions and they will provide specific hypotheses about how to modify their behavior moving forward. Then, track progress.

If you are on a team with someone motivated to Make It Work, they will love it when you ask them to help you solve a problem. Don't be afraid to seek their advice, but also don't be surprised when they spend all evening thinking about and solving your issue. Also, realize that they are likely to quickly identify the problem in any idea you present to them. Don't take this personally, but know that they are simply doing what they're wired to do. Similarly, if you are managed by someone motivated to Make It Work, know that they will tinker with your work until they are satisfied that everything is as it should be. They might exhibit more control than you'd like, so be candid with them about how their involvement is affecting your work. It can help to say, "Would it be possible for me to spend a week on this first, then let you help me finish it up?" or "Could I come up with a few options to pitch to you at our next meeting?"

Where They Thrive

PROJECTS WITH A CLEAR PROBLEM TO SOLVE

They are fixers by nature and driven to identify root causes and remedy them. Any job or project with a clearly defined problem will keep them engaged, such as diagnosing and fixing a client's IT issues or figuring out why the turnover rate is so high in the Finance Department. However, once the problem is solved they will quickly move on to the next thing, and if they are in a role without many clear problems, they might cause instability and insecurity by perpetually blowing things up just so they have something to fix. A job with a steady stream of new problems to solve is their best fit.

TURNAROUND ROLES

If a company needs fixing, they are your person. They are good at stepping into a broken system, team, or organization and getting it back on course. They can quickly spot the issues and propose solutions. They draw energy from the cause of righting the ship, and will continue to bring their best until they feel things are stabilized again. Then they will begin seeking a new challenge. They are typically not the person to continue leading the organization once it's back on course.

ANALYTICAL AND INVESTIGATIVE ROLES

They have the drive to sift through a lot of information, seeking hidden gems of insight that will unlock the solution to a vexing problem. They thrive in positions requiring diagnosis and deep research, such as IT or mechanical roles, investigative accounting, or financial analysis. Additionally, they are often skilled at offering non-intuitive creative solutions based upon their investigation or analysis, and in mobilizing others toward implementing them.

20: DEVELOP

You are motivated by the process of building and developing from start to finish.

Ella couldn't figure out why her work life was suddenly so draining. She had recently been promoted into a role she'd always dreamed of—running PR and communications for a division of a large publicly traded company. However, despite loving most aspects of her job, she just didn't find her new position to be nearly as satisfying as she'd hoped. Just a few months earlier, she'd been among the rank-and-file of the department where she was handed important projects, had to develop concepts and pitch them, and in many cases was the person delivering the communication to the media or an internal client. Her favorite projects were those where she was involved from the identification of the problem or need right up through the final delivery.

As she reflected on her previous role, she realized that she'd unlocked the secret of her discontent. Her new, more managerial position required her to be involved at certain key points of a project, like the very beginning and maybe the end to sign off, but didn't allow her to be directly involved in doing the work itself. Instead, she was now a layer or two removed from the actual tasks. The reason for her discontent was that Ella is deeply motivated to Develop, a function that her new role did not require of her. With this newfound understanding, Ella was able to take ownership of a few projects per quarter and see them through from beginning to end, which both activated her Motivation Code and allowed her to have a better understanding of what was happening within her department.

Process Oriented

Those motivated to Develop are driven by the step-by-step process of developing or building something from start to finish. They are most engaged when involved in the entire process, rather than stepping into and out of it over time. They enjoy seeing how the end result of their work reflects all the stages, processes, and procedures that brought it to its final form. They enjoy the process of putting all the pieces together in the developmental flow.

Involved from Start to Finish

It's very important to them to be involved from the very beginning of the project. They want to be immersed in the vision, the strategy, the execution, and the completion. If they are not involved in any one of these stages, they will find the work less motivating. It's not only projects they want to engage with from conception to conclusion, it's also their leadership of people (they are much more engaged if they are involved in the hiring decision and then developing and promoting someone rather than taking on someone else's hire), the development of processes, or even building something more concrete like an office space.

Highly Practical

They can achieve real, measurable results because of their direct involvement in the work. They are highly practical and delight in any progress. They love to start up new initiatives, and will see them through to the end, even when asked to move on to other work. Once they've committed to an effort, they want to see it through, and if they are pulled from it they will struggle to move on.

People Person

They are often also talented at developing others, because they stay committed to the relationship and the other person's goals long after others might give up. This means they are often highly empathetic managers, and are prone to being the "person behind the person" as others climb the ladder of success.

The Shadow Side

Because of their need to be involved throughout the life of a project, there are a few shadow side attributes that the Develop person must be mindful of.

THEY MIGHT BUILD OR EXTEND THINGS BEYOND WHAT'S NECESSARY

Because of their drive to develop, they are always seeking ways to make things better or improve their present state. As such, they might continue development long after everyone else thinks it's good enough. If they manage others, this can lead to frustration on the team, as members are ready to move on to other, more pressing work while the Develop manager is still obsessing over how to improve last month's project.

THEY INSIST ON BEING HANDS-ON AT EVERY STAGE

It's very important to them to be directly involved with the development of the project, organization, or system. They need direct input into decisions, and being involved in carrying out those decisions is even better. To those around them, this can come across as excessive control and can squelch the independence and creative drive of those doing the work. They might assume a "just tell me what to do" mind-set over time, which means the team will not perform up to its potential and talent retention can become a challenge.

CONSTANT DRIVE FOR NEW DEVELOPMENT STRETCHES RESOURCES TO THE MAX

They might want to continually invest in developing something within their area of responsibility, even though it's good enough for everyone else. For example, if they are an IT manager in charge of the servers for your organization, they might be driven to continuously develop the server system, replacing parts of the network and striving to grow it over time even beyond what's needed. This can strain the budget and create unnecessary stress within the organization.

MIGHT EXHIBIT A FAILURE TO ENGAGE IN NEEDED
MAINTENANCE ACTIVITIES

Because they are typically focused on what's next and building toward the future, those driven to Develop might neglect the very necessary maintenance activities that keep systems and organizations running effectively. If it doesn't feel new, or like something is being built or developed, they don't have much interest in spending their time or energy on it.

Working with a Develop Person

KNOW THAT THEY WILL TAKE INSTRUCTION WELL,
BUT MUST FEEL FORWARD MOMENTUM

Because of their drive to continually build on past attempts, it's important for them to see how your instructions or guidance will lead them toward new development in their personal or professional life. They don't live in the here and now, so you must frame your leadership in terms of where a particular set of instructions or bit of advice will help them go if followed. Contextualize your advice in terms of development work they are already doing so it feels part of something they've already been working on.

HELP THEM DELEGATE

Identify areas where they are overly involved in decisions that should be handed off to others, or places where they might be stifling the creative insights of others because they are smothering the team with their excessive involvement. Work with them to establish a leadership philosophy or set of guide rails to direct the team, and challenge them to step away from control and instead operate from a place of influence. One way to do this is to simply ask them about what they are working on and specific tasks they plan to accomplish in the coming week. If you sense they are doing tasks that should be delegated, challenge them on that and push them to invite others to take ownership of the work.

IDENTIFY AREAS OF EXCESSIVE INTERPERSONAL DEVELOPMENT

At times, they can become overly concerned with the development of others. This can look like over-involvement in another's professional development plan, making decisions for them, or pushing them to take on projects they don't have the bandwidth to do well. Ask the Develop-motivated individual about how they engage with others in their life, and about any aspirations or goals they have for the people they interact with. Look for areas where they might be layering ambitions onto others that are unfair, unreasonable, or serve their own purposes, not those of the people they are supposedly helping.

REFRAME MAINTENANCE ACTIVITIES IN DEVELOPMENTAL TERMS

As mentioned above, they are unlikely to be recharged by routine or maintenance-oriented activities. For example, instead of doing the maintenance themselves, perhaps they can develop a system to help them do so. Or they can break the maintenance activities into small chunks of work to see each smaller piece in terms of developmental activity rather than an ongoing list of repeatable actions with no goal other than sustaining.

If you are on a team with someone driven to Develop, know that they will want to be involved in every stage of the project, from beginning to end. Invite their participation at these key moments, and allow them to take ownership of the parts of the project where they have the most energy. Also, be aware of areas where they might overdevelop and stretch the team's resources to the max. If you notice they seem to be spending too much time on a particular area of a project, don't be afraid to challenge them or ask why.

Where They Thrive

ROLES WHERE THEY ARE INVOLVED FROM BEGINNING TO END

They are energized by being part of the conception, strategy, and execution of a project, all the way through to its completion and celebration. They want to be directly involved in development throughout; if they are required to jump in and out of the work, they will be less energized. If they can be hands-on from beginning to end, they will do their best work and be most engaged.

DESIGN ROLES

They perform well when they get to conceptualize then oversee the implementation of their ideas. So roles like architecture, graphic design, or others that allow them to be involved throughout the process, from idea to execution, will feel gratifying to them. Any job that allows them to dream things up then build them will be work they tend to love.

LEADING HIGH-GROWTH ORGANIZATIONS

They are propelled by growth, and love to build on what was there before. So an organization that's expanding or needs someone to lead the charge into new markets or opportunities will find them well suited to the task. They are motivated to see their new initiatives through to the end and will not allow opportunities to wither due to neglect.

21: ESTABLISH

You are motivated to lay secure foundations and become established.

Over the years, when I've been given a new opportunity or I'm starting a new business venture, I turn to Jacob. He is quick to identify the first steps I need to take, often illuminating opportunities or issues I'd not even considered. In fact, we had a great conversation one evening about this book and the motivation-related work we do at Pruvio. He offered some foundational advice regarding how we should think about our product offerings, how to build the business so it will still be viable in ten years, and how to ensure we laid the proper groundwork to prove our credibility to CEOs and boards, with whom he routinely works. The reason I seek Jacob's advice is because he exhibits the qualities of someone motivated to Establish. He knows how to build things properly from the start, while balancing the desire to move quickly and pursue an ambitious vision.

Foundation Layers

Those motivated to Establish want to lay secure foundations, and to become established. They are not interested in quick fixes or temporary solutions, but are instead motivated to construct the groundwork for something that will stand the test of time. When they can point to a project years later that they helped build, they are deeply fulfilled.

Must See the Purpose

It's important to them that the purpose or plan for what they are establishing is well defined. If they don't understand why something is being asked of them, or can't understand the path to building it, they are less motivated to engage. They want to work with proven methods and reputable people. They have little interest in speculation or taking big leaps into the unknown. Rather, they want to be involved with teams and organizations that have a track record of excellence and success, and who understand the importance of getting things right from the beginning as the foundation for a long-lasting venture.

Want to Be a Major Factor

It is not necessarily important that they are the key player in any given effort. They don't get their drive from being "known" for something. It's enough for them to know they were a major factor in an effort, and that what they've built alongside others will continue to have lasting impact for a long time to come.

Trustworthy and Reliable

They tend to be very trustworthy, loyal, and reliable. They are committed to you and to the team. You don't have to worry about ulterior motives or nefarious intent. They will stick with you, the purpose, and the plan until they see it through.

Can Assess Effectiveness of a Plan

They are also a great gauge for whether the plans you've made are reliable and founded upon proper principles. Because it's so important for them to know that everything lines up and is stable from the start, they are reliable team members to entrust with new projects and initiatives; there's little concern they will overlook the small, important details necessary at the beginning of a venture.

See It Through to the End

They tend to finish what they start, and tie up all loose ends. They don't leave half-finished projects in their wake. They might move slowly to ensure that everything is done properly, but they will always see it through to the end.

The Shadow Side

Establishers make certain that everything is done properly, but there are a few shadow side attributes that they must manage.

THEY TEND TO BE RIGID AND INFLEXIBLE, AND GET STUCK IN THE GROOVE

Once they have a direction in mind and have settled on the "proper way" forward, it's very difficult to convince them otherwise. It might take a while for them to make up their mind and determine the right direction, but once they settle on a path they won't waver from it.

THEY TEND TO BE LATE TO INNOVATE

Because they are focused on tried-and-true methods and technologies, they might be late to the game with regard to new innovations. They might need help understanding why new ways of doing things are equally or more effective than the way they've been doing them for years.

THEY HAVE LITTLE EMPATHY FOR STRUGGLING UNDERPERFORMERS

So much of their life is about delivering on objectives and finishing what they start that they have a difficult time understanding how someone can see the world differently. When a team member doesn't perform well or seems to lack the sense of urgency necessary to get things done, the Establish-motivated individual might ignore or disconnect from them relationally. Or they might simply pressure the teammate to get the work done, regardless of their struggle.

THEY ARE UNWILLING TO FOLLOW UNPROVEN LEADERS OR DIRECTIONS

Because it's important for them to follow well-established pathways and proper procedure, they initially mistrust new leadership or changes of plan. It can take them a bit of time to come around to a new approach, and they might require additional convincing before they are on board. However, as stated above, once they're with you, they are all in.

Working with an Establish Person

When interacting with them, it's important to understand that their skepticism does not reflect mistrust of you or your ideas. Rather, they need to know that what you're presenting is right before they will endorse your suggestions.

PRESENT THE EVIDENCE BEHIND YOUR IDEAS

When sharing a new idea, show them the models, examples, and data that lead you to believe it is valid. Shortcut straight to proving that your idea has a good foundation and has been used by others before to accomplish similar objectives.

BE CLEAR, LOGICAL, AND STRAIGHTFORWARD

Don't use metaphors or poetic language. Rather, speak directly to them and help them see the logic in your idea. If they sense you are speaking around the topic rather than straight to the heart of it, they will grow skeptical and you will lose them. Enter the conversation prepared to give it to them straight.

SHOW YOUR CREDENTIALS

They need to know that you've done it before, and that you can do it again. Don't be afraid to tell them about your experiences and how those past efforts apply to your current projects and ideas. They want to know your methods are proven and they can trust your instincts.

ONCE IT'S EARNED, GIVE AND EXPECT LOYALTY

As mentioned above, it might take a while for them to fully trust you. However, once you've earned their trust, know that you'll have it moving forward. In turn, give them your loyalty and assume the best. Know that they will be working for your betterment, and the organization's.

Where They Thrive

EARLY-STAGE WORK WHERE FOUNDATIONS ARE BEING LAID

They are motivated to get things right from the beginning, and to ensure that loose ends are tied up before moving on. Therefore, they are often excellent people to rely on when you absolutely need things done properly, so the foundation won't crumble once you begin to build upon it.

ANALYZING PARTNERSHIPS, CONTRACTS, OR NEW WORK

They can quickly gauge whether something is reliable. Their drive to seek the truth of a situation and determine if things add up can serve an organization well when working with a new partner or considering bringing on a collaborator. They are motivated to see where there are natural sympathies of interest and where the parties are misaligned, and to seek ways of bringing confluence to the situation.

WORK THAT ALLOWS THEM TO SEE THEIR DIRECT IMPACT

They don't care if they are the central player or recognized for their contribution, but they must be able to see that the work they did had an impact on the final results. If they are simply adding marginal value throughout a project and it's not very visible in the finished product, they will lose energy quickly. However, if they can clearly see how their thought, direct involvement, and persuasive voice shaped the results, they will find the work satisfying.

THE OPTIMIZER FAMILY: SUMMARY

Those motivated by Optimizer Family themes keep your team functioning at peak efficiency. They will ensure that there isn't value slipping through the cracks. However, they also need interesting and important problems to focus on in order to stay engaged with their work.

If you are motivated by one of these themes, here are a few tips for structuring your life and work for maximum effectiveness:

Learn to Recognize When Something Is an Actual Problem Versus a Problem in Your Own Mind

It's tempting to see fixable problems everywhere when you're motivated to Optimize. Train yourself to recognize when a problem is something you should truly focus on and when it's simply a nuisance with little bearing on the overall effectiveness and efficiency of the organization. Don't get caught rearranging the deck chairs on the *Titanic*!

Recognize That Others Are Not Necessarily Interested in Improvement

It can be frustrating for you to see areas for improvement in others' lives that they have absolutely no interest in addressing. That's not your issue. Instead, focus on problems you can actually fix. If you are their manager, focus on helping them better understand *why* they should address underperforming areas rather than simply pushing them to do it.

Practice Allowing Others to Take Ownership

One of the struggles for many people motivated by themes in the Optimizer Family is that they tend to try to overcontrol the work of others, and they want to maintain a level of ownership in what's happening around them. Practice releasing that control instinct, and instead focus on the handful of projects and problems you can actually influence in a significant way. Focus on helping those you lead and collaborate with to develop their own abilities and instincts, and strive to help them unleash their own best work.

Break Your Work into Short-Term, Easy Wins

You likely measure your progress by how many problems you fix, or how efficiently something is running. Over the long term, this can feel daunting and overwhelming. Make sure you break your efforts into manageable, short-term objectives so you don't struggle to feel you're making reasonable progress.

Chapter Eight

THE KEY CONTRIBUTOR FAMILY

Common Characteristics

- Wants to be at the center of the action
- Derives energy from being recognized for their contributions
- Driven to show how they're unique from everyone else on the team
- Finds motivation in growing their influence and ownership of teams and processes

SOME PEOPLE ARE BORN TO BE IN THE SPOTLIGHT. THOSE WHO FIND themselves drawn to being onstage, at the center of attention, in the middle of wherever the action is, are often driven by a Key Contributor Family theme. They are often very talented and unique in their thoughts and approaches, and they tend to be the ones who bring clarity to a situation, organize the work, and get things moving along in the effort to create a remarkable outcome. They also want to highlight their personal—and often incisive—input. Clear about the comparative differences between themselves and others, they tend to be competitive and want to control outcomes.

There are six key motivational themes within the Key Contributor Family:

1. Evoke Recognition
2. Bring Control
3. Be Unique
4. Be Central
5. Gain Ownership
6. Excel

22: EVOKE RECOGNITION

You are motivated to capture the interest and attention of others.

Kristie is a brilliant marketer. Over the past several years, she separated herself from her peers and was promoted into increasing levels of responsibility, until she was finally given the ability to start her own division within the company. Along with her promotion came a huge pay raise and a lot of flexibility. She was allowed to hire anyone she wanted, and to structure the team and project load as she saw fit. It was a dream job.

Last fall, she was given a prestigious company award recognizing her for her contributions. Her manager took the stage and shared five minutes of solid praise for Kristie, touting all her accomplishments and praising her loyalty to the company. To Kristie, the promotion, the flexibility, and the trust she'd earned from her organization meant far less than those few words from her manager. In fact, prior to that evening, she'd been feeling a little down about how things were going. After the praise from her manager, she was on cloud nine and ready to take on the world. This is a classic example of someone motivated to Evoke Recognition.

Excited to Receive Attention for Their Work

Those motivated to Evoke Recognition are driven to capture the attention and interest of others. They do their best, most engaged work when they are operating with high visibility and their contribution is noticed by those they are working with or for. They want an audience and to gain increasing visibility for their efforts. They are often quick to identify angles that will help them attract more attention, and will wait until the right time to ensure maximum visibility for their work. They are most motivated when there is a reaction to what they say or do. When they work in a silo or vacuum, they might struggle to stay motivated. Also, they might accomplish something significant, but if there is no audience for it, or if it's not recognized, they will not find it nearly as motivating as the work they are recognized for. So if given a choice, they will always gravitate toward the work that will give them more attention or augment their reputation in some way.

Because they are easily able to identify areas of maximum exposure, they often bring attention to the organizations or people they represent. They can also shine the spotlight on others, and often increase awareness of whatever they are involved with.

Drawn to the Spotlight

They are typically comfortable with the pressures that come with high-profile roles. They are willing to shoulder the public eye, even though they might occasionally complain about it. They gravitate toward roles seen as glamorous or prestigious or that allow them a baked-in audience.

Born Performers

They also often have strong performing and influencing abilities. They shine when given a chance to show what they can do, and frequently stand out from those around them in a competitive field. Additionally, they are able to persuade and influence others because of their charm and ability to perform whatever role is needed to accomplish the goal.

The Shadow Side

Because they are drawn to and tend to live in the spotlight, there are a few shadow-side attributes those driven to Evoke Recognition must be mindful of:

THEY MIGHT LACK SELF-POSSESSION

So much of what they do is for an audience, so they can easily lose their sense of who they are in the world and what they truly stand for. Marilyn Monroe often discussed "belonging to the world," or a sense that she did not exist for her own sake, but for the sake of the public. Often, everything in the life of the person motivated to Evoke Recognition is about performance and putting on a face for the world. Monroe's photographers noted that she especially shone in front of the camera, but tended to slump when the shoot was over.

THEY TEND TO HOG THE SPOTLIGHT

Because they are driven to gain an audience for their work, they will quickly position themselves at the center of attention. This might cause them to exaggerate their role in a project to get the credit they crave, or take more than their share of minutes in a presentation so they are seen as the key player in the meeting. Either way, those around them could feel edged out by their need for attention.

THEY NEED CONSTANT RECOGNITION, REGARDLESS OF THE CIRCUMSTANCES

They thrive on attention, so expect that they will seek feedback from you (and those around you) constantly. In some ways, they only truly know how they are doing from others' reactions. Don't be shy in offering your thoughts and praising their work. It will keep them alive.

They are overly concerned with their personal reputation and very sensitive to how others perceive them; any slight can send them into days of rumination. If they don't think you like them, they will work hard to win you over. If they underperformed in a public setting, they will replay the incident in their head for weeks, thinking of how they could have done better. It's very important to them that their reputation be impeccable and their contribution seen as valuable.

THEY TEND NOT TO RECOGNIZE OTHERS FOR THEIR CONTRIBUTION

When working collaboratively, they might overlook the work of others that allowed the project to succeed. Instead, they see their contribution as central, and believe that without them it never could have happened. This isn't selfishness, and it's not a conscious power play. Rather, it's simply a function of where they get their motivational energy.

Four Ways to Encourage an Evoke Recognition Person

- Recognize their accomplishment in front of the team. Be specific about what they did.
- Write them a note of personal encouragement.
- Allow them to be the lead presenter for the team's work.
- Send an email to your manager praising their work, and copy them on it.

Working with an Evoke Recognition Person

RECOGNIZE THAT THEY MIGHT FEEL EMBARRASSED BY THEIR NEED TO BE IN THE SPOTLIGHT

It's likely they are aware of their need to be at the center of attention, but to them it feels as natural as taking on a necessary but undesirable task. It's best not to directly call out their behavior, but to instead ask them questions about how that behavior affects those around them. For example, if they took more than their share of time in a meeting, you could ask, "Do you think Julie had enough opportunity to present her portion of the idea?" By engaging them in a conversation, you can help them identify how their spotlight-seeking might be affecting their teammates and short-circuiting the work of the team. Additionally, remind yourself and them that motivation is a gift, not a curse. Yes, it can lead to undesirable outcomes, but their desire for the spotlight can yield tremendous dividends for both themselves and the organization. Never paint their behavior as selfish, but instead help them think through when it's best activated and when it's best left to simmer.

GIVE THEM CHANCES TO SHINE

When possible, allow them the opportunity to step into the spotlight. When these opportunities are not claimed but instead freely granted by the team or organization, they will most certainly rise to the occasion. Let them give the presentation, introduce the reorganization, or do the interviews and PR work. They will relish the opportunity.

SHOWER THEM WITH RECOGNITION

Don't be shy with praise. They will come alive when encouraged and given the attention they so crave. Don't just toss them insincere compliments, though. They are savvy enough to recognize when you're piling on the BS. Instead, seek ways of highlighting their work and putting them in the spotlight. It won't take much to fire them up. Any opportunity to shine will play directly to their motivation.

Where They Thrive

PUBLIC-FACING ROLES

They want to be the front person, the recognized face, the name on the marquee. It's important their contribution is recognized, even if they were only marginally attached to a project. They are fine with stepping in at the last minute and presenting the work of the team, and are often excellent at doing so. They will be less motivated by work performed in isolation, or where they will be largely invisible.

PERFORMANCES

They often gravitate toward acting, music, theater, and other high-profile public roles. They are fine with the pressure, recognizing that it comes with the turf. They can intuit how to make others laugh, cry, or sing, and are good at reading the room, whether they are performing in a play or presenting a rebranding strategy to the C-suite.

TEAMS WHERE THEY HAVE A VOICE

They are energized when they work in an environment that allows them to express ideas. They want to know that their voice is heard and attention will be paid to their opinions. If they sense their input is not welcomed or their ideas are unappreciated, they will naturally gravitate to places where they can take center stage, whether or not it's appreciated.

23: BRING CONTROL

You want to be in charge and in control of your own destiny.

There were two distinct philosophies that drove computer manufacturers of the 1970s and 1980s. One camp believed that computing platforms should be open and allow other manufacturers to plug in to them or modify how they function so computers could be customized to each user's needs. The other camp, led by Apple and its cofounder Steve Jobs, believed that computing systems should be closed, and that the manufacturer should maintain control of every aspect of a computer's functioning, from design to the software that runs on it. Jobs was renowned for his attention to detail, and even required that the interior design of his machines match the beauty of their exterior. In his official biography, *Steve Jobs*, Walter Isaacson wrote, "One of his core principles was that hardware and software should be tightly integrated. He loved to control all aspects of his life, and the only way to do that with computers was to take responsibility for the user experience from end to end." This is the core expression of someone motivated to Bring Control.

Driven to Pull the Strings

Those motivated to Bring Control want to be in charge of their own destiny and areas of activity. It's important to them to feel they are steering their own career and decisions, that no one is pulling the strings. Independence is imperative, and they do their best work when given an objective and allowed to figure out their own path to accomplishing it.

Assertive

Generally, they tend to be very assertive, especially when leading a team. They struggle with needing to micromanage and control every aspect of the team's work, and might stifle the team's creativity if left unchecked. Because of this, they enjoy having authority to make decisions, move resources around, and assign work as they see fit to accomplish objectives according to their own design.

Confidence Boosters

Because of their assertiveness, they tend to raise the overall confidence level of the organization. They project a kind of certainty when they make decisions, and this gives the people around them a sense of stability. They are unafraid to proclaim what they believe will happen next, even when others around them can't believe it's possible.

Able to Bring Clarity

They are able to bring order even in difficult and chaotic situations. When others tend to shrink back in uncertainty, they are willing to step in and take charge. They have a gift for dealing with ambiguity, so they are not threatened when things don't add up. As a result, their confidence allows them to inspire loyalty from those they lead, and they are often the unifying voice of the organization, even if they aren't officially in charge. Because of this, their presence may be perceived as a threat to organizational leaders who are differently gifted.

The Shadow Side

While their ability to own and shape the work can be valuable to the team, there are also some potential shadow-side attributes of this motivation to watch out for:

THEY CAN BE OVERLY AUTHORITARIAN AND DIRECTIVE

To those motivated to Bring Control, whatever is necessary to move things into alignment with their vision is perfectly acceptable. They can be ruthless in their feedback and methods, and often lack empathy for those who can't seem to "get it." Along with this, they can often treat others as mere extensions of their will. They don't count the personal cost of their actions, but instead simply do whatever is needed to persuade others to do what they themselves believe is best. While this tactic can be effective in accomplishing their objectives, it tends to alienate others.

THEY ARE RARELY SWAYED BY OTHERS' OPINIONS

They can become locked into their own way of thinking, and they see others' arguments as a threat to their view of reality. They will sometimes come around to the views of others if they are able to integrate the new way of thinking with their own, but not if it requires a complete change of mind.

THEY FIND IT HARD TO ADMIT MISTAKES

Instead, they will attempt to rationalize why their failure was actually a success, or to try to paint a picture of how a setback is a temporary blip on the way to a much bigger victory.

THEY CAN DRIVE THEMSELVES AND OTHERS TOO HARD

Because achieving the objective according to their personal vision is their ultimate aim, they will use whatever resources or people necessary to accomplish it. They will drive people to their limit, and will even work themselves to the edge of burnout in order to make progress. They can be relentless in their feedback and demand perfection from the people they lead. Anything less is seen as a slight to their own vision and reputation.

Working with a Bring Control Person

DON'T BACK DOWN

You earn their respect and trust by standing firm in your opinion. If they perceive you are waffling, they will see it as a sign of weakness and discount your thoughts and ideas. Operate by principle. Agree to disagree when necessary.

CLARIFY BOUNDARIES AND EXPECTATIONS

Don't allow them to walk all over your personal space. Set clear boundaries around your time, and hold firm to them. Additionally, make sure your relational expectations are clearly set, and defend them whenever you feel there is a breach. If the Bring Control–motivated individual treats you poorly, tell them you don't appreciate it and you expect them to exhibit more respect. If they call you at 10:00 p.m. about a project, remind them you have a personal life and you'll be happy to discuss their ideas in the morning.

DISCUSS THE IMPACT OF THEIR BEHAVIOR WITH THEM

Help them to see that their excessive drive to control, while yielding positive results for the organization, can also yield negative relational results if left unchecked. Tell them how their behavior is affecting you and the rest of the team, and allow them to problem-solve and help determine a path forward. Always allow the idea to be theirs, because they are much more likely to follow through if it is.

DON'T HOLD MISTAKES AGAINST THEM

When they inevitably get something wrong, don't hold it over them. Instead, talk about a path forward. If you help them see that admitting a mistake gains trust from the very people they need to work with to accomplish their objectives, they will be much more likely to do so. Don't bring up their past errors in conversations about future efforts.

Where They Thrive

JOBS THAT ALLOW THEM TO DO THEIR OWN THING

They don't want to be prescribed a course of action, but want to figure out their own path. Roles that allow them the flexibility to figure it out as they go will give them the most energy. Independence is the most desired quality in a team setting. They tend to do well as entrepreneurs, and especially as solopreneurs, where they are the only one calling the shots.

CHAOS

They bring a level of clarity and confidence to others in the midst of uncertainty. They tend to thrive in roles that allow them to step into confusion and bring a bit of direction. Because of this, their teams are often very loyal, because they calm the fear of not knowing what to do. However, they can also overstep and micromanage, which can lead to frustration and dysfunction. Generally, they are willing to step up and lead when others are fearful.

ORGANIZATIONS WITH CONFIDENT LEADERS

Their clarity and ability to move in and take charge can feel like a threat to insecure leaders. Therefore, they might find they are in constant power struggles with managers afraid of being encroached upon. However, if their leadership is secure and confident about the Bring Control person's abilities, it's a recipe for deep motivation and successful work.

24: BE UNIQUE

You seek to distinguish yourself by displaying some talent, quality, or aspect that is distinctive and special.

Everyone is unique. We each have a blend of personality traits, strengths, interests, and—of course—motivations. However, the Be Unique motivation isn't just about recognizing the originality in all of us. Individuals with this theme in their Motivation Code seek to distinguish themselves from others by displaying some talent, quality, or aspect that is distinctive and special. They desire to set themselves apart from others by highlighting their uniqueness. While many people *are* distinctive, they aren't necessarily motivated to highlight those areas of uniqueness in the way the Be Unique–motivated person is. These people are fundamentally interested in personal performance that distinguishes them.

Eager to Be Noticed

Those motivated to Be Unique don't do well when they blend in with the crowd. They will attempt to create contrasts with other people through what they wear, do, or say to highlight how they are unique. They dislike conformity, and will often attempt to stand out by doing the ordinary in an extraordinary way.

Source of Many Ideas

Because of their desire to do things in a new and unique way, they are a fountain of novel ideas when current practices are tired and worn out. They often promote innovative methods that benefit the entire organization.

Willing to Take a Stand

They are also willing to stand against the tide, especially when their nonconformity means holding fast to their ideals. They won't simply go with the flow to keep the peace. You will always know what they think, because they are vocal about their point of view.

Open to New Ways of Thinking

Their desire to be unique can often pull the entire team into new and unexplored territory. While differently motivated team members might prefer to play it safe or value progress over everything else, the Be Unique–motivated person will challenge teammates to explore atypical ideas, will question assumptions, and will push the team to stand out from the rest of the organization. This might create some discomfort among collaborators, but it often yields surprising and valuable results.

The Shadow Side

Their desire to Be Unique allows these individuals to offer fresh perspective and spark intriguing conversation, but can also lead to a few shadow-side attributes:

THEY CAN BE CONSISTENTLY CONTRARIAN

Because so much of their motivation comes from drawing the contrast between themselves and others, they often adopt an argumentative persona by default. This can make it difficult to move forward on even the simplest tasks, as they might exhibit a need to be different just for the sake of it, not because it's actually helpful to the process.

THEY COMPARE THEMSELVES TO OTHERS

Those driven to Be Unique draw their motivation from where they stand in relation to others, which means they must be scanning the environment at all times to note those differences. This can lead to unnecessary comparison and obsession with uniqueness at the expense of effectiveness. (Sometimes the most obvious solution is best.)

THEY TEND TO HAVE UNREALISTIC IDEAS AT TIMES

Their nonconformist tendency can lead them to dream well beyond the bounds of reality, putting pressure on teammates to be the voice of reason. In these situations, they might adopt a "persecuted artist" attitude, signaling that others simply don't value their unique ideas.

THEY SEEK CONSTANT RECOGNITION FOR THEIR DISTINCTIVENESS

They can become an energy drain on their leader due to their constant need for feedback and recognition. They might resent others when they don't feel they are getting the attention they deserve.

Working with a Be Unique Person

Collaborating with someone motivated in this way can be a bit of a roller coaster. Because they react against others, they might take one position on a given day, then completely reverse when it feels like the tide is heading in that direction. Be patient and appreciate the uniqueness they bring to the team and the work. Here are a few principles for doing so:

EXPECT THE UNEXPECTED

Know that they are going to throw you curveballs, and the better prepared you are to deal with them the more likely your collaboration will thrive. Don't get upset with them for pushing boundaries, but instead remind yourself they are simply operating within their motivational energy.

BE WILLING TO STRETCH BEYOND YOUR NORMAL METHODS

Perhaps you aren't motivated in the same ways as the Be Unique person, but are instead more comfortable with tried-and-true methods. Remind yourself going into any meeting with them that there could be value in challenging assumptions and trying new ways of thinking about the work.

CHALLENGE THEIR NONCONFORMITY

When their unwillingness to go with the flow is having a detrimental effect on the team, don't be afraid to point it out. If you are gracious and accommodating when their nontraditional ideas are helpful, they will likely return the favor when you point out the effects of their behavior in an appreciative, understanding way.

GIVE THEM FLEXIBILITY TO APPROACH THEIR WORK AS THEY SEE FIT

Don't stick them in a routine role with specific expectations for process and productivity. They might be capable of doing the work, but they will be miserable. Instead, strive to give them freedom in how they approach the work as long as they deliver results. Give them bounded autonomy, freedom within limits.

Where They Thrive

ROLES THAT ALLOW FOR SELF-EXPRESSION

They come alive when given the opportunity to distinguish themselves from their peers. Conformity is their mortal enemy, as is the blue-suit-striped-tie uniform of many professions. They crave a job that allows them to speak their mind and prove how unique they are. Therefore, they often thrive in creative roles or those that reward original and even risky thought.

CREATIVE LEADERSHIP ROLES

They are often a fountain of new ideas and energy for projects. Others around them feed off that energy, and it can drive a team in directions they wouldn't have considered otherwise. Therefore, these individuals are often good as leaders of teams that have to challenge the tried-and-true, and must routinely carve new paths for themselves and their clients.

JOBS THAT ALLOW PERSONAL DISTINCTION

They want to stand apart from the crowd, so any role that allows their personal performance to be recognized and rewarded is likely to be energizing to them. If their job is largely team based with little room for individuals to make their unique mark, it will not motivate them as deeply. However, if they are able to show they not only contributed to a project, but their contribution was unlike anyone else's and could only have been accomplished by them, they will feel deeply satisfied with the results.

25: BE CENTRAL

You are motivated to be a key person who holds things together and gives them meaning and/or direction.

Some people are motivated by a need to be at the center of the action. They get their energy from calling the shots, holding things together, or providing clear direction for everyone else on the team or project. The driving force for them is knowing they were in the room where it happened and can show they were an integral part of key decisions and initiatives.

Excited to Be Close to the Action

You are likely to find those motivated by Be Central at the inner sanctum of the organization. They tend to gravitate toward roles allowing them to be near where all the action and decision making happens. They will seek opportunities to be close to those in power, and find meaning in being at the hub.

Eager to Be Called upon First

They also desire to be the person called upon when it matters most. They find it important to know—and to have it known—that they were a critical factor in the success of a project. Being the go-to person gives them a lot of energy. However, sometimes their energy comes from knowing their contribution was crucial, even if only a few people are aware. The important thing for them is understanding that it couldn't have happened without them.

Power Hungry

They also sometimes desire to be important to a person at the center of power. They bend their life and work around ensuring that this person has what they need, and that they are the one who can provide it for them. Simply being close to the center of where decisions are made, and influencing those decisions, is what gives them energy.

Critical to the Success of the Team

Those motivated to Be Central are often critical to the success of the organization or individual they serve. "I couldn't have done it without them" is the praise they most crave. Because of this, they are trustworthy people who aspire to earn and live up to the mantle of responsibility placed upon them. Because of their unique purview, at the center of the action, they are also often capable of seeing how things are coming together, and have the unique ability to deal with complexity and navigate the needs of multiple areas of the organization.

The Shadow Side

Because they are driven to shoulder heavy responsibility at the center of the action, there are a number of watch points for those driven to Be Central:

THEY CAN EASILY BURN OUT OR OVEREXTEND THEMSELVES

They want to serve, and they heed the call when an opportunity arises. However, their drive to remain at the center of things can cause them to overwork in ways that affect their health and focus. They are not good at saying no, but instead will do whatever it takes to deliver results.

THEY MUST BE ASKED OR CALLED UPON BEFORE TAKING ACTION

Because they want to know that their actions are critical to success, they will often wait until someone calls upon them before they act. They don't initiate big ideas or projects unless they know it is important to someone in the midst of the action.

THEY CAN ENABLE CODEPENDENT RELATIONSHIPS

Because of their need to do whatever it takes, they can sometimes attach themselves to a leader who will take advantage of their tremendous commitment and work ethic. This can enable unhealthy organizational behavior and dysfunctional leadership if not attended to.

THEY SEEK REINFORCEMENT OF THEIR VALUES

They might also need to have their importance reinforced regularly. They need others to see that they are important—at the center of the action—and that nothing could happen without their contribution.

Three Ways to Engage a Be Central Person

- Invite them into a small, important meeting.
- Ask their opinion about an important decision, especially if it affects the entire team or organization.
- Call on them first when asking for ideas or opinions.

Working with a Be Central Person

Because they are so driven to do what's necessary to get the work done and to be trusted and reliable, you have to keep your eye on the overall health and well-being of a Be Central–motivated person.

ASK ABOUT OVERWHELM

It's typical that those motivated to Be Central will take on too much, and possibly even get to a point where they are unable to take on important work because they are spread too thin. They might also feel overwhelmed but unwilling to admit it because they are afraid if they show they can't handle the pressure they'll be replaced. It's important to help them understand the difference between their very helpful drive to be at the center of the action and the unhealthy need to *always* be at the center of the action.

KEEP YOUR EYES ON AREAS OF CONFLICT

It's very possible they will try to do more work than they are capable of, and in a team context they might lack the desire to delegate, or they might hold on to information that could be valuable to other members. If this is a pattern, it can create conflict as others feel they aren't being given the opportunity to shine. The Be Central–motivated individual might also not contribute in needed ways if they don't perceive their role as being central.

ASK QUESTIONS, DON'T GIVE COMMANDS

Allow them to determine the right course of action rather than telling them what to do. This will give them the sense they are the key influencer of decisions, not just a pawn in your game. It's important for those motivated to Be Central to feel they are driving the conversation, not sitting in the passenger seat.

DON'T BE OVERLY CONSTRICTIVE WITH ACCOUNTABILITY

People motivated to Be Central often chafe at attempts to hold them accountable to metrics. It's not because they don't value performance, but because they feel their commitment to the team and their centrality should be enough to affirm they will do what's necessary to succeed. They might feel insulted if you layer accountability measures upon them that feel overly controlling, or that are perceived as questioning their loyalty. Instead, work with them to develop measures they can live within and that they feel are a reflection of their commitment to the team.

Where They Thrive

ROLES THAT ALLOW DIRECT INPUT INTO DECISIONS THAT SHAPE THE WORK

They must see that they are close to the core of the organization, and crave having direct input into important decisions. They want to know they are central to the efforts of the organization, in success or failure. It's important for them to feel like it couldn't happen without them.

HUB ROLES

They want to be the nerve center of the work, and thrive when information and decisions flow through them. This doesn't mean they need to be in a significant leadership role, though it can. It does mean they need to be a clear hub at the center of communication, workflow, and decision making about important projects or work. If they are kept out of the loop, they will disengage.

CROSS-COLLABORATIVE ROLES

Because they are drawn to the center of the action, they often see connections across various parts of the organization that others might overlook. They can spot patterns, potential efficiencies, ways of collaborating, and dots to connect that can improve projects and processes. They thrive when they are the go-to person who stands between two parts of an organization or process.

26: GAIN OWNERSHIP

You are motivated to acquire what you want and to exercise ownership or control over what is yours.

For some people, just having influence isn't enough. They are driven to acquire what they want and to exercise ownership or control over what is their own. They tend to be collectors, gatherers, and savers. The important aspect is that they feel ownership and clear boundaries related to what's theirs and what's yours. It's very important to them that they have a lot of latitude over their areas of responsibility.

Daniel wasn't just a good real estate agent, he was beloved by his clients. Mostly, he was the go-to person for the entire east side of the city. He'd begun his work by focusing on one small neighborhood, but over time he had made a game of chipping away at surrounding neighborhoods, advertising in key publications and seeking referrals from satisfied clients, until he had become the best known agent within twenty miles of his office. However, he wasn't finished. Now he's set his sights on the west side of the city, and has already begun to advertise and grow his presence there. Truth be told, he probably won't stop until he is the dominant player in the entire city. Daniel is driven to Gain Ownership.

Masters of Their Domain

They want to be the master of their domain, and will often embrace the role of provider. They take great satisfaction in sharing what they've collected or acquired with others who inhabit that domain. They will be generous with others, but they don't want to feel like their ownership is threatened in any way.

Eager to Acquire

Many wealthy people are driven by the need to Gain Ownership. They are constantly on the lookout for more companies to acquire or ways to grow their "kingdom" of influence. Constant growth in terms of the breadth of their ownership and depth of control they exercise within it is their primary driver.

Goal Focused

They tend to be very goal focused and determined. They know what they want, and they aren't afraid to go after it. Their goals are often specific and measurable, because they have defined targets in mind—for example, the manager who wants to move an entire operating division under her authority, or a real estate developer who sets his sights on a specific property. They will not rest until they've acquired ownership of that which they desire.

Loyal Protectors

Along with their drive to acquire ownership, they often feel a strong sense of loyalty to people who fall within their domain. They assume a deep sense of responsibility for their well-being, and take it personally when someone doesn't feel they are being looked after properly. They are very detail oriented, and seek to ensure that those within their areas of responsibility believe they have their best interests at heart.

Stakeholders

It's important to them that they have a sense of ownership over the final product at the end of any process. It's not enough to simply be part of a team. If they can't point to their direct influence, and even feel ownership of the key decisions and final results, they will not be nearly as satisfied with the work.

The Shadow Side

Gain Ownership–motivated individuals can be growth catalysts and drivers of organizational purpose, but due to their focus on growing their sphere of ownership, there are a few shadow-side attributes to watch out for:

THEY CAN BE POSSESSIVE AND TERRITORIAL

They draw clear boundaries around what's "mine" and "yours," and when they feel someone is encroaching on their domain, they can be brutal about defending their turf. For example, another manager making an ask of someone on their team might seem like a small matter, but to those driven to Gain Ownership it can become the opening shot of World War III. It's important for those working with them to ensure they are in the loop on decisions that affect their areas of responsibility.

THEY TEND TO VALUE MATERIAL POSSESSIONS

Because they desire to acquire more and more, they can tend to focus on measuring the size of their domain by the value of the possessions they own. They look to concrete metrics to help them determine how they're doing, and the easiest of these is the size of their bank account, how much their car cost, or how impressive their home is.

THEY TEND TO HOARD

Their drive to acquire can play out as an impulse to purchase items attractive to them. This doesn't necessarily mean their home is filled with boxes of old newspapers. It can instead look like a large collection of (never-used) fountain pens or notebooks, or a vast closet full of shoes.

THEY CAN'T PAY ATTENTION BEYOND THEIR DOMAIN

They are much less interested in decisions that don't directly affect the areas under their control. Because of this, they might miss bigger patterns playing out around them, or ignore important organizational decisions that will ultimately impact their team.

Working with a Gain Ownership Person

DON'T THREATEN THEIR OWNERSHIP

It's important to build trust and help them see that you don't intend to encroach on their areas of responsibility. This is especially important when you are new to a team or organization and they see you as a person with potentially suspicious motives.

RESPECT BOUNDARIES

Set clear and defined expectations and boundaries around your collaboration, and make sure you communicate anytime you think you might need to cross one of them. Consider how your decisions will affect their "domain" before putting your plans in motion. Clarify your responsibilities and theirs, then stay in touch about whether expectations are being met.

GIVE THEM AGENCY TO DETERMINE THEIR OWN PATH

Don't prescribe courses of action. Instead, give them problems to solve, and allow them to bring resources from within their domain to bear against them. Allow them to own both the problem and the outcome. If they don't, they will withdraw and wait for you to tell them what to do.

POINT OUT AREAS WHERE THEIR CONTROL IS STIFLING THE TEAM

They might be unable to see how their tendency to exercise deep influence over those within their domain is creating bottlenecks in the process.

After all, in their mind they are functioning with everyone's best interests in mind. They might need someone to help them identify ways they can release a bit of control and allow teammates to also exercise ownership over the work. Otherwise, it's difficult to retain talented people on the team for long.

Where They Thrive

LEADERSHIP ROLES

Because they are driven to acquire increasing responsibility and control, they often thrive when they are responsible for helping an organization grow its presence in the marketplace or acquire other organizations doing sympathetic work. They will spot opportunities to increase their sphere of ownership in areas others might overlook.

TERRITORIES

They will be energized by work that allows them to dominate a territory, such as sales roles where they are competing with other organizations for the business within an area, or where they are able to increase their influence within a defined part of an area they are charged with overseeing.

ROLES WITH POTENTIAL FOR MORE AUTHORITY

They also gravitate to roles where it's easy to see how to be promoted into greater levels of ownership and authority. They want to know how to increase their purview, and are much more interested in that than in other rewards like pay and flexibility. They want to grow their stature within the organization and have more sway over how decisions are made within their area of ownership.

27: EXCEL

You want to stand above the rest or, at the very least, do your absolute best as you exceed the performance or expectations of those around you.

The movie *Talladega Nights* stars Will Ferrell as an accidental race car driver named Ricky Bobby who ends up succeeding in spite of himself. In the movie, Ricky is haunted by the words of his father during an elementary school career day: "If you're not first, you're last." Those words compel him to desire victory at all costs, and anything less than a first-place finish is unacceptable. As ridiculous as it might be to compare a fictional movie character to the real world, that mantra—"If you're not first, you're last"—could very well apply to those driven to Excel. They are motivated to do their absolute best as they pursue their objectives. Simply accomplishing the objective is not sufficient if they don't feel they performed at their peak in the process.

Competitive

They tend to thrive on competition. They strive to conquer everything they take part in, and can sometimes turn noncompetitive activities into a struggle for dominance. They are also motivated by others with equal skills. They flourish when trying to outdo others in their pursuit of excellence.

Able to Exceed Expectations

They want to go above and beyond the simple requirements of their work, responsibility, or position. They will do what they deem necessary to exceed the expectations of others. They want to be the best, the fastest, the most. It's important to them to know they have dominated the closest competition.

Ambitious

They are typically very goal focused, and aim high. They aren't interested in doing the normal things that others settle for. They will choose the hardest objective, the biggest challenge, the riskiest venture, and they won't be comfortable until they've accomplished what they set out to do.

Standard-Bearers

Because they tend to reach for big goals, they also tend to raise the standards and expectations of those around them. This is especially true if they have a secondary motivation of Team Player. They can bring excellence to the entire team and refuse to allow others to settle for less than a completely flawless performance. They are self-starters and don't require close management. They are committed to their work, and are results oriented. They know how to determine whether they succeeded or failed without someone else qualifying their work for them.

The Shadow Side

Those driven to Excel tend to challenge others around them to raise their game and can push the organization to new heights, but there are a few shadow-side attributes to watch for:

THEY CAN CREATE UNHEALTHY COMPETITION

As can be expected, because they typically need to feel a sense of competition in order to thrive, they can introduce competition in areas where it doesn't belong. Simple team meetings can turn into all-out wrestling matches, or people who would generally collaborate freely will begin hoarding information to gain an advantage in the race for the next promotion. This can cause disharmony within the team environment.

THEY CAN BE HARSH ON THEMSELVES AND OTHERS

Because of their exacting standards, they can sometimes be unforgiving of lapses in performance. They also turn these standards upon themselves and demand nothing but excellence in their own work. They beat themselves up over small mistakes others wouldn't even notice.

THEY FIND IT HARD TO ENGAGE UNLESS THEY CAN BE THE BEST

Vince Lombardi, likely an Excel-motivated person, once quipped that being second place is meaningless. This means that many people motivated this way won't even accept a task unless they believe they can be the best in the world at it. If they sense they might fail, they will do whatever they can to pass it on to someone else.

THEY MUST WIN AT ALL COSTS

At times, the need to Excel can cause them to do things they otherwise wouldn't. In extreme cases, this can lead to unethical behavior. Or it could mean needing to belittle others to position themselves as superior. In their world, "whatever it takes" can become a life mantra.

THEY TEND TO OVERESTIMATE THEIR ABILITIES

Additionally, they might underestimate the skill actually necessary to accomplish the big objectives they've placed before themselves. The need to stretch themselves can cause them to overestimate their own abilities or ignore signs they aren't up to the task. Instead, in unhealthy cases, they will rationalize why they failed and blame others, the circumstances, or anything other than their own shortcomings. Failure is not an option for them.

Three Ways an Excel Person Can Become Overstretched

- They fail to accept positive results if they are not number one, and fail to rest until they achieve the top spot.

- They compare their present work with something excellent the team did years ago, and keep restarting because they can't replicate it.

- They seem to arbitrarily raise the bar for performance every time even though no one expects them to.

Working with an Excel Person

IDENTIFY UNREALISTIC EXPECTATIONS

It's likely they are reaching well beyond what's reasonable, and that can have effects on you and everyone else they work with. While their drive to perform is beneficial to the team overall, as discussed above it can lead to impossible goals and burnout. When necessary, draw distinctions with them between what's possible in the near term versus what might be possible in the longer term. Help them understand how their demands are affecting everyone else.

MAKE IT EASY FOR THEM TO WIN

Not easy in the sense of how difficult the project is, but easily *measurable*. Establish clear metrics that allow them to distinguish whether they are succeeding or failing, and benchmarks that help them track their progress against others. (For example, "Most people can only finish one proposal a week, but I suspect you might be able to do two. Possible?" They will try to do three.) Don't patronize them—they will easily discern when you are—but definitely give them clear targets.

DEFINE SUCCESS AS HELPING OTHERS WIN

If you can help them see that their competitive spirit can be applied to unleashing others' best work, they will embody superlative leadership. They will commit to making their team or collaborative group the best equipped and most focused and engaged in the organization. And others' success will raise the standards surrounding them, which is one of their core desires.

COMMIT TO MEETING THEIR REASONABLE STANDARDS

If you want to earn their respect and attention, you must hold yourself to a standard of excellence. If they perceive you don't have high standards for yourself, they will be unlikely to listen to any advice or correction you offer. They want to be around others who—like them—believe that excellence is a way of life.

DON'T GET CAUGHT IN THEIR COMPETITIVE STREAK

As mentioned above, they will try to turn even the most innocuous acts into a competition. Don't get swept up and distracted by their constant need to compare. It doesn't matter. Let them find their motivation in whatever form it takes, and be grateful for the way it elevates the performance and standards of the team.

Where They Thrive

HIGHLY COMPETITIVE FIELDS

They want to show they are successful, as measured against others, so roles allowing them to gauge their success tend to be more motivating. Sales is a wonderful example, because it tends to be measured very concretely and allows them to set ever-increasing targets.

WORK THAT ALLOWS THEM TO SET THEIR OWN GOALS

They are self-starters and do well when given latitude to direct their own work. They don't need someone micromanaging them, and might even disengage if they feel their manager is too directive.

JOBS WITH UPWARD MOBILITY

They measure their success against themselves as much as the competition, so they want to do work allowing them to set ever-higher standards and continuously improve their performance. To excel, they need to feel they are reaching beyond their grasp.

THE KEY CONTRIBUTOR: SUMMARY

Those whose Motivation Code contains themes within the Key Contributor Family have incredible force of will to push things forward. You'll usually find them at the front of the pack challenging everyone to take on the next project, even in the face of insurmountable odds. Overall, the value they provide is incalculable.

If you are motivated by one of these themes, here are a few tips for structuring your life and work for maximum effectiveness:

Recognize That Your Motivation Is a Gift

Don't feel guilty that you need to be at the center of things to stay engaged—it's how you're wired! Remember that your drive to be in the middle of the action has both positive and negative qualities, and learn to monitor your shadow sides so they don't detract from your positive and productive qualities.

Apply Your Motivation to Help Others

Find ways to use your motivation to lift up and motivate the people around you to do their best work. Challenge them to up their own game, and use your drive to Excel to raise the standards of the entire organization, but with empathy for those who don't think like you do.

Find Your Core Team

You need people around you who can speak truth, identify areas where you are veering off course, and show you ways you are losing your identity in your work. Choose two or three people with such insight into your life and give them permission to tell you what they see, without being defensive. They should be people with your best interests at heart, or who have "skin in the game." Most important, try to find these people well before you need them, so they are able to see patterns in your life over a period of time before they help you make a big decision.

Recognize That Some Work Just Has to Be Done

Not everything you do will result in recognition. Therefore, acknowledge those moments when you are ignoring the more behind-the-scenes, but no less important, responsibilities because you aren't motivated to tackle them. Instead, remind yourself that private successes are a way of preparing yourself for the public ones. By doing so, you will learn to direct your motivation in ways that are helpful to your overall productivity.

PART III

NOW WHAT?

Chapter Nine

LIVING OUT YOUR MOTIVATION

BEFORE WE DIVE INTO HOW YOU CAN APPLY YOUR NEWFOUND KNOWL-edge of Motivation Code, it might be useful to recap what we've just covered. Below are each of the twenty-seven themes listed within their family.

Visionary	Achiever	Team Player
1. Achieve Potential	4. Meet the Challenge	8. Collaborate
2. Make an Impact	5. Overcome	9. Make the Grade
3. Experience the Ideal	6. Bring to Completion	10. Serve
	7. Advance	11. Influence Behavior
Learner	**Optimizer**	**Key Contributor**
12. Comprehend and Express	16. Organize	22. Evoke Recognition
13. Master	17. Make It Right	23. Bring Control
14. Demonstrate New Learning	18. Improve	24. Be Unique
15. Explore	19. Make It Work	25. Be Central
	20. Develop	26. Gain Ownership
	21. Establish	27. Excel

Now that you better understand what makes you tick, it is *very* possible for you to:

1. Activate your Motivation Code more consistently and in a way that allows you to implement your unique motivations to the work you're already doing.
2. Negotiate for opportunities to engage in tasks that more naturally align with your Motivation Code.
3. Spot opportunities that aren't currently on your radar, but that are in line with your drives.

Of course, there is no such thing as a job perfectly suited to you in every way. Every job has aspects you may not enjoy. But the life-changing power of knowing your Motivation Code is that now you will understand why you are so drained when you have to go to that team meeting, collaborate with others for that long-term project, or complete rote work with little room to explore new ideas. Knowing the *why* will illuminate your path to a better-suited situation.

Here's the key point: it is not selfish to want to operate within your Motivation Code. In fact, it's the least selfish thing you can do, because it means you will be more deeply engaged and create better value more consistently. The most selfish thing you could do may be to collect a paycheck week after week knowing you're just faking it. The problems the world now faces, from the political and economic to the social and environmental, will not be solved by halfhearted people doing halfhearted work. We need people fully engaged—now more than ever!

WHERE YOU GET YOUR ENERGY MATTERS

Although your Motivation Code is made up of your top motivational themes, this doesn't mean you are impervious to the influence of other motivations. For example, if Collaboration ranks at the bottom of your list, you might still be able to work with others just fine. It simply means pulling together teams to accomplish goals isn't where you get your motivational energy. Similarly, just because you score high on Be Central, it doesn't mean you will never enjoy work unless you're at the center of the action.

Your Motivation Code describes where you derive your motivational energy, and explains what makes certain activities and situations deeply gratifying. The more you operate within that Motivation Code, the more likely you are to find your work meaningful and to persist in the face of adversity and resistance.

As mentioned above, the themes that comprise your Motivation Code often work together to serve one dominant motivation. This is especially the case if you have one outlier motivational theme that scores far above the others. For instance, in my case, my top motivational theme (by far) is Make an Impact. My number two and number four motivations are Meet the Challenge and Overcome. (Number three is Influence Behavior.) In my life, I am interested in meeting challenges, influencing behavior, and overcoming only in so much as it allows me to make an impact, which is my dominant motivation. If there is no impact on the lives of others or the world around me on the other side of that challenge, I am far less motivated to undertake it. So while the drive is internal (Meet the Challenge, Overcome), the results I'm seeking—and that motivate me—are external (Make an Impact).

As you begin to understand your top motivational themes, you will see how they've played out in your life and work in patterns over time. For example, I am very likely to accept work that allows me to help underdogs overcome the odds, such as with small firms taking on the industry giant or a company trying to come back from an almost-fatal economic event. I am drawn to movies about people who overcome a great obstacle, like *Rudy*, *Gladiator*, or *The Pursuit of Happyness*. Some of my best work has been with the "little guy" taking on the world. This is my Make an Impact motivation playing out, in concert with a Meet the Challenge driver (because I want to do something big) and an Overcome chaser (because I love it when the odds are stacked against me). If you want to fire me up, tell me about an initiative where I can influence others, that will make a tangible difference in the world, started by an underdog under attack from defenders of the status quo—I'm in!

LOOK AT THE PATTERNS

Take a look at your Motivation Code report. Now take a few minutes with pen and paper and consider the following questions:

1. Where do you see your Motivation Code at work? As you think about the kinds of tasks you've enjoyed taking on in the past year, write down instances when your Motivation Code was activated.
2. Now think about the tasks you found less gratifying. Was there a disconnect between the work and your Motivation Code? Write down any instances where you felt bored, dissatisfied, and generally unmotivated, and consider why that might have been.
3. When are you most energized? When are you most drained? How might these situations relate to your top motivation? Write down a few key, notable interactions you've had with others over the past few weeks and consider how your Motivation Code may have affected them.
4. Imagine the work ahead of you. How might you knowingly activate your Motivation Code to create an environment in which you are more engaged and driven to shine?

This is an exercise to evaluate how your Motivation Code affects your choices and behavior. Your Motivation Code can be a lens through which you filter interactions and decisions, so the more you can stop and consider how it shapes your behavior, the more likely you will be to make decisions that align with what truly motivates you, and to squelch shadow-side behaviors before they affect others.

CRAFT YOUR JOB

Few of us get to do only the tasks we enjoy all day. To be completely frank, I don't *love* writing, and I say this as an author who's written five books in ten years—that's hundreds of thousands of words and well over a decade of research. But look at it this way. My top themes are:

1. Make an Impact
2. Meet the Challenge
3. Influence Behavior

Can you think of a better role for someone with this Motivation Code than writing books and speaking about them? I get to engage in the very challenging work of writing books so I can influence the people who interact with my work and make an impact on the world around me. So for me, the difficulty of writing books is outweighed by the Motivation Code that makes the work thrilling and propels me forward.

This is why the advice "follow your passion" is often so misguided. We take this to mean that we should focus on pursuing only the tasks we enjoy doing. But that's not an accurate way to understand passion. As I wrote in my book *Die Empty*, the word "passion" is derived from the Latin *patī*, which means "to suffer." So when we talk about following our passion, what we should mean is to pursue outcomes for which we are willing to suffer if necessary. ("Follow your suffering" doesn't quite have the same ring to it, huh?)

I believe this is also a helpful way to think about your Motivation Code. What truly motivates you does not equate to doing what you love. Rather, it's about understanding which outcomes matter so much to you that you're willing to endure undesirable tasks to accomplish them. If your top motivation is Collaborate, you may be willing to put up with the messiness of relational conflict to achieve the satisfaction of working together as a team. If your top theme is Explore, you may be willing to endure discomfort as you step out into the unknown and chart new territory. If your top theme is Overcome, you may do whatever is necessary to defeat the enemy and bring justice.

Therefore, think about your work not in terms of the job you do, but in terms of the value of the outcomes you achieve—this is where deep engagement and gratification comes from. This is what it truly means to "follow your passion."

> **Exercise: Develop a Motivation Statement (30 minutes)**
>
> Now that you know your Motivation Code, it's time to craft a Motivation Statement to remind you of those core drivers as you go about your daily work. Your Motivation Statement is a brief sentence that describes you at your best by taking into account your top three motivational themes. It looks like this:
>
> > "I am fundamentally motivated to _____ as I _____ and _____."
>
> Go through the descriptions of your top motivational themes in the previous chapters and highlight some words or phrases that resonate with you. Then, craft your Motivation Statement and place it somewhere visible as a way to remind yourself of what drives you.
>
> For example, here is my Motivation Statement:
>
> > "I am fundamentally motivated to *put my mark on the world* (Make an Impact) as I *rise to the challenge* (Meet the Challenge) and *change how people feel or think* (Influence Behavior)."

TALK WITH YOUR MANAGER ABOUT MOTIVATION

Once you begin the process of evaluating how your role and responsibilities do—or do not—align with your Motivation Code, you may find yourself looking for ways to operate more consistently within your sweet spot. For some people, this may require seeking a new job in an entirely different industry—and that's okay. But more often than not, there's no need to switch careers. If much of your daily work runs counter to your Motivation Code (for example, if you spend most of your days crunching numbers in a cubicle alone but your top motivation is Collaborate), start by having a conversation with your manager about how you might better approach your responsibilities in a way consistent with what drives you.

Discussing your Motivation Code with your manager takes careful planning, so here are some tips for making this exchange a productive one:

Approach the conversation as a teacher, not an employee. Share with your manager what you've learned about your Motivation Code and how it's helped you understand where your engagement and motivational energy come from. Talk about your Motivation Statement and how it frames up the kinds of work you've found deeply gratifying, and how the outcomes you pursued in those situations overshadowed the tasks you had to engage in to achieve them. You might say something like, "I always knew I loved to explore new topics, but never realized how core it was to job satisfaction. Can I share with you a little about how I'm driven to Comprehend and Express?"

Give an example of a recent moment when your work was fueled by your Motivation Code. Tell your manager about a project, an interaction with a coworker, or a leadership moment that was fueled by your Motivation Code and discuss how the outcome might have been different if you were otherwise motivated. Then, be honest about how you might activate your Motivation Code in other aspects of your job.

Give an example of a recent moment when you were operating outside of your Motivation Code. Share a story of when you were tasked with work that was difficult for you because it ran contrary to your

Motivation Code. For example, if Collaborate is your top theme, or Team Player is your top family, being stuck in a back office cranking through proposals on your own was probably extremely draining. You probably did a great job, but it's not the kind of work you'd prefer to do every day. Eventually, you'd burn out.

Suggest ways to intentionally shape your role around your Motivation Code. Come to the conversation with a few practical action steps you could take to integrate your Motivation Code into your work each day. For example, you could say, "I know I am driven to Make an Impact, but much of my work is currently done in the background. Would it be possible for me to have one or two longer-term projects to own, that I can work on with others, that will allow me to directly see the results of my efforts?"

When discussing all this, make certain to do it through the lens of what's best for the organization, not just what's best for you. You need to make the case that a fully engaged, alive, and activated you is going to produce more value for your stakeholders, your clients, and your teammates.

Five Reasons Why Your Manager Should Care about Motivation

- It improves retention and increases job satisfaction.
- Operating within Motivation Code increases the degree of discretionary energy team members spend on work.
- Awareness of others' motivations will improve collaboration and decrease unnecessary conflict.
- Better alignment of tasks and natural motivations means deeper organizational engagement.
- When people feel understood, they feel more psychologically safe within the team.

CLEAN FUEL AND DIRTY FUEL

In our universe, energy is conserved, meaning that when you burn something, you release that potential energy into the world, where it can be harnessed. For millennia, humans have burned wood, brush, and eventually fossil fuels to keep themselves warm, cook food, and even hurtle through time and space in rockets going hundreds of miles per hour.

However, not all the fuels we use are clean. Some of them burn dirty. They leave by-products. When we burn coal or wood, they leave soot and ash. And when we burn fossil fuels, they release gases into the atmosphere that can cause harmful side effects to life on earth.

In the same way, I believe we need to be mindful of the fuels we burn to motivate our work. All too often, these fuels burn dirty. Anger, seizing ownership, proving your worth at all costs, putting others down, and extracting what you can: these are "against" fuels, meaning they fundamentally oppose someone or something else. They fuel us to right some personal wrong from the past instead of focusing on creating possibility. They cause us to hold grudges. Yes, they may produce the energy needed to get through our work, and maybe even to achieve our goals, but they leave behind residue on those with whom we interact, and on ourselves: bitterness. And when bitterness takes root, it makes engagement, creativity, and generosity very challenging. We begin to see other people as the enemy rather than assuming the best of them. Bitterness bounds possibility, because the only options available to us are those that direct our creativity against our enemies.

When we are working against something, we will never fully feel gratified, even when we have success. We might need to continuously tell the story of how we bested someone else. We might need to remind ourselves over and over that we didn't get the last word. We might need to stir up our anger toward others as we tackle new projects. Instead of focusing on the positive impact we want to make on the world, we become obsessed with vanquishing those we feel have wronged us.

"Save every rejection letter and use it as fuel!"

"Channel your anger into your work!"

"Show them who they're messing with!"

I hear this kind of well-intended advice handed out frequently, especially to young aspiring artists and entrepreneurs. Like most advice, it seems profound on the surface, and actually works for some people—for a while. However, I believe this kind of dirty fuel is poorly conceived. Striving to prove others wrong will work temporarily. But once we've done that, what do we have? What motivates our work when we're stuck on one side of an argument? With that mind-set, we will always need another enemy to stay motivated.

The truth is, our fight to prove others wrong is born out of a fear that they might be right, that maybe we aren't actually good enough, that we aren't worthy of being on this stage, in this room, or on this team. When we strive to gain acceptance from someone who has rejected us, the reality is that the acceptance we crave is our own.

In the end, no level of achievement can ever quell the internal whispering of:

"You're not good enough."

"It's never going to be good enough for them."

"You don't belong here."

That's why we need to choose clean fuels to motivate our work. Motivation Code is the cleanest fuel I've discovered. Because it's unique to each of us, it's the best way we can make our personal contributions to the world while also feeling alive, engaged, and fully present. Operating within what naturally drives us allows us to work toward the outcomes we most crave.

Who are you working *for*, not *against*? What change are you creating every single time you choose to sit down and do the work? What outcomes motivate you so much that you're willing—if necessary—to suffer for them? This is the purest form of *true* motivation.

The most profound work you will ever do will be accomplished only when you are burning clean fuel. I believe this happens when you operate squarely and consistently within your Motivation Code. The world needs you to be fully alive, fully engaged, and fully yourself. And as you move forward in hope and possibility, uniquely driven to contribute to this world, your impact will resound.

Acknowledgments

This book and the research it represents is the result of decades of work by dozens of people.

Thank you to the partners at Pruvio: Tony Kroening, Peter Larson, Art Miller III, Randy Zimmerman, Joshua Miller, Todd Hall, Brian Williamson, Mark Herringshaw, Jeff Burton, Todd Henry, and Rod Penner. Also, thank you to everyone involved with SIMA International for more than fifty years. We acknowledge in a special way the late Arthur Miller Jr, developer of SIMA (System for Identifying Motivated Abilities), which grounds and orients Motivation Code. Thanks to our Motivation Code coaches network, especially those coaches who contributed thoughts to this book, including Joe Cavanaugh and Jonathan Paul.

Thanks to our brilliant editors Niki Papadopoulos and Nina Rodriguez-Marty for your excellent work and for knowing how to motivate us to keep going. Also, we're deeply grateful to Adrian Zackheim and the entire Portfolio team for your faith in this project, and to our agent Melissa Sarver-White at Folio Literary Management for helping navigate this book to market.

Finally, thank you to our families and loved ones for your patience and for believing in our work.

Appendix A

ADDITIONAL RESOURCES

We have developed a number of resources to help you go deeper in your understanding of Motivation Code and to implement it with your organization. All of these resources are available at MotivationCode.com.

PERSONAL ASSESSMENT SUITE

In addition to the free assessment mentioned in the book, we offer a complete assessment with a suite of exercises, a full ranking of all twenty-seven motivational themes, and additional video resources to help you deeply integrate Motivation Code into your life and work.

Also, we can connect you with a network of Motivation Code certified coaches who are trained to help you better understand your top motivations through an Impact Session.

TOOLS FOR ORGANIZATIONS

We offer Motivation Code workshops, keynotes, and a software platform to help managers monitor the motivation of team members and unleash engagement and productivity. We can also arrange assessments for your full team, and conduct Impact Sessions for the entire organization.

PRACTITIONER CERTIFICATION

If you would like to become certified to use Motivation Code in your coaching or to lead Impact Sessions with your team members or clients, we offer a certification program and a library of resources to help you.

Visit motivationcode.com to learn more.

Appendix B

MOTIVATION CODE'S TECHNICAL DEVELOPMENT & VALIDATION*

Todd W. Hall, PhD
Joshua Miller, PhD
Peter Larson, PhD

INTRODUCTION

Motivation Code is an online, self-report assessment of core motivation that identifies the top motivations that represent an individual's strongest natural drives. In addition, Motivation Code provides scores and rankings for all twenty-seven motivational themes. Although the assessment is a self-report and provides quantitative results, it integrates a narrative methodology with a quantitative methodology. We believe it to be one of the first commercial assessments to accomplish this important breakthrough.

The 162 items of Motivation Code were based on fifty years of theory and research from the System for Identifying Motivated Abilities

---

* This is an abbreviation of the full Motivation Code Technical Report available for download at motivationcode.com/science. Motivation Code was previously known as MCORE.

(SIMA), a semistructured interview and coding system for identifying an individual's core motivations. The SIMA system has been used by SIMA International Inc. for the purposes of executive search, selection, employee engagement and development, and vocational development.

Motivation Code has been developed according to current psychometric standards. This report presents evidence of reliability and validity gathered to date, in accordance with *The Standards for Educational and Psychological Testing* (American Educational Research Association, American Psychological Association, and National Council on Measurement in Education, 1999). Primary applications of Motivation Code for vocational development, employee engagement, leadership development, and team development are briefly discussed.

SYSTEM FOR IDENTIFYING MOTIVATED ABILITIES (SIMA): A VALIDATED FOUNDATION FOR MOTIVATION CODE

The System for Identifying Motivated Abilities (SIMA) is an important foundation for Motivation Code because the twenty-seven motivational themes of Motivation Code were identified through the SIMA process. This analytical process, developed by Arthur Miller,[*] is based upon clients' stories of activities they have deeply enjoyed and performed well. These "achievement stories," drawn out by interview and/or client autobiography, are then analyzed by a SIMA biographer who identifies within them a pattern of motivated behavior that is both innate and unique.

When it was first utilized in 1961, SIMA was a purely idiographic process; each client's motivational pattern was developed through anal-

---

[*] Miller and his colleagues have written a variety of books about SIMA and its impact in helping people be more productive and fulfilled. For example: Arthur Miller and William Hendricks, *The Power of Uniqueness* (Grand Rapids, MI: Zondervan, 2002); Dr. Nick Isbister and Dr, Martin Robinson, *Who Do You Think You Are?: Understanding Your Motives and Maximizing Your Abilities* (New York: HarperCollins, 1999).

APPENDIX B: MOTIVATION CODE'S TECHNICAL DEVELOPMENT

ysis of his or her own achievement narrative. However, after tens of thousands of individual pattern reports, SIMA biographers in the 1980s began to identify recurring themes that they captured in a taxonomy of motivational elements. This thematization introduced a nomothetic dimension to the SIMA process, which enabled it to be thoroughly validated according to the American Psychological Association (APA) testing standards.

The SIMA taxonomy provides the twenty-seven psychometric constructs of Motivation Code, which are called motivational themes. Since the taxonomy was introduced, the process and themes have been validated in a number of formal studies.* One of the most important was The Leadership Profile Project, carried out from 1989 to 1990 by Dr. John Crites, one of the leading vocational psychologists of the twentieth century. The objective of the research was to evaluate the usefulness of SIMA for identifying potential leaders for executive and managerial positions. The research design followed test standards established by APA in 1985 for determining the psychometric characteristics of assessment techniques (i.e., scoring objectivity, reliability, and validity).

Dr. Crites conducted seven studies to assess the extent to which SIMA met APA standards for psychometric soundness. He concluded that SIMA was both theoretically sound and empirically reliable and valid for use as a selection tool. He found that it met all applicable APA standards for the assessment and selection of leaders, and that an individual MAP® profile is stable over time.

Motivation Code builds on these studies because it is thoroughly grounded in the SIMA process. However, it is also a new approach, blending the narrative dimension of SIMA and its taxonomy of central motivational themes with traditional forms of psychometric assessment.

---

* The *SIMA Theory & Research Handbook* is available upon request. This includes a bibliography of books, articles, and dissertations relevant to SIMA's validity.

MOTIVATION CODE'S THEORETICAL BASIS IN CONTEMPORARY PSYCHOLOGY

There is growing consensus, particularly within disciplines that focus on human behavior, that narrative provides deep insight for understanding people and for helping them make sense of their lives. Narrative Psychology has become a vital sub-discipline of psychology proper. A foremost thinker in this emerging new field is Dan McAdams. He and a colleague recently wrote that:

> Contemporary narrative approaches have made much more explicit the ways in which storytelling shapes self-making.... It is with respect to narrative identity ... that personality psychology's commitment to showing how every person is like no other person is most readily accomplished. Every life story is unique. The rich texture of human individuality is best captured in the intensive examination of the individual life story.*

Motivation Code (and the SIMA process that grounds it) is distinctive among contemporary assessments because it is drawn explicitly from a client's unique life story. This makes it consonant with the aims of narrative psychology but also distinct from other forms of psychometric assessment, which begin not with the client's own story, but with a slate of pre-established options.

Another burgeoning movement that confirms both the methods and the objectives of Motivation Code is that of Positive Psychology, defined by two of its founders, Martin Seligman and Mihaly Csikszentmihalyi, as "the scientific study of positive human functioning and flourishing on multiple levels that include the biological, personal, rela-

---

* Dan McAdams and J. L. Pals, "A New Big Five: Fundamental Principles for an Integrative Science of Personality," *American Psychologist* 61 (3): 204–21.

tional, institutional, cultural, and global dimensions of life."* Seligman also argues that positive psychology orients people to what he calls "the good life," which is "using your signature strengths every day to produce authentic happiness and abundant gratification."† Motivation Code uncovers the innate motivated gifts of people by studying the key moments of their positive functioning in order to help assure authentic happiness in their life, and therefore it is highly consistent with positive psychology.

DEVELOPMENT OF MOTIVATION CODE

As mentioned previously, SIMA biographers during the 1980s began to identify recurring themes that led to a taxonomy of motivations. This introduced a nomothetic dimension to SIMA that was the first step in developing Motivation Code. The goal was to use SIMA themes to develop an online, cost-effective, quantitative assessment. However, in order to retain the power of narrative in the assessment, we combined narrative and quantitative methods in a way that produces quantitative results.

MOTIVATION CODE: INITIAL DEVELOPMENT

The development of Motivation Code began in 2013. Four open-ended text questions were used to obtain four distinct achievement stories from participants. The developers worked with senior SIMA biographers to identify the most prominent motivational themes from the SIMA taxonomy. This led to the identification of twenty-seven motivational themes to be included in Motivation Code. The developers then

---

* M. E. P. Seligman and M. Csikszentmihali, "Positive Psychology: An Introduction," *American Psychologist* 55(1) (2000): 5–14.
† M. E. P. Seligman, *Authentic Happiness* (New York: Free Press, 2009).

translated these themes into statements on which individuals could rate the degree to which an item was satisfying to a particular achievement story.

MOTIVATION CODE: CURRENT VERSION

Results from the early data analysis over nearly two years led to the current, commercially viable version of Motivation Code (see below for a discussion of reliability and validity). Six items per motivational theme were included, which increased the internal consistency (reliability) of the themes. Two items are displayed for each of three achievement stories. Licensed SIMA biographers authored and approved each item.

The Likert-type scale was also revised, which produced more reliable scales. The "Does not apply" rating is now scored as missing data (so it does not affect the mean score for the theme), and an additional rating was added to retain a five-point Likert scale. The revised Likert scale ranges from: 1—Not satisfying; 2—Slightly satisfying; 3—Moderately satisfying; 4—Very satisfying; and 5—Most deeply satisfying.

Two separate data sets were analyzed to examine the reliability and validity of Motivation Code. The first data set was a national data set collected through a survey panel. The second data set was drawn from the Motivation Code database of clients who took the assessment from February 2015 to June 2015. The results from each study are described below.

RELIABILITY

The reliability of a scale score is an estimate of its stability, or that part of the score that is not due to random error. There are two main types of reliability: internal consistency and test-retest reliability. Internal consistency is the most common type of reliability used, and we report on this below.

APPENDIX B: MOTIVATION CODE'S TECHNICAL DEVELOPMENT

Internal consistency is typically evaluated using Cronbach's alpha. Cronbach's alpha measures the extent to which all the variables on a scale are positively associated with one another. It is an adjustment to the average correlation between every item and every other item. The alpha is also the average split-half reliability coefficient for all possible splits. A split-half reliability is found by randomly selecting half of the items in a scale, computing the mean to create a composite variable, and then creating a composite variable of the remaining half, and correlating the two composite variables. The expected value for the random split-half reliability is alpha. J. C. Nunnally offered a rule of thumb of 0.70 as the cutoff for "acceptable" internal consistency, as shown in Table 1. By definition, scales with fewer items will have lower alphas.

Table 1

Cronbach's alpha (α)	Internal consistency
.90 to .99	Excellent
.80 to .89	Good
.70 to .79	Acceptable
.60 to .69	Questionable
.50 to .59	Poor
Below .50	Unacceptable

J. C. Nunnally, *Psychometric Theory*, 2nd ed. (New York: McGraw-Hill, 1978).

Two data sets were analyzed, as mentioned above. For data set one, gathered from a national panel of 347 individuals, the overall alphas were very strong. As Table 2 shows, all twenty-seven scales exhibited alpha coefficients above the conventional cutoff of .70, and fifteen scales were in the .80 to .89 range. The mean alpha across all twenty-seven scales was .80, demonstrating strong overall internal consistency.

Table 2

Motivation Code DATA SET 1: NATIONAL VALIDATION STUDY

Alpha Range	No. of Scales in this Range
.70 to .79	12
.80 to .89	15
Mean alpha of all 27 themes	0.80

The second data analysis, conducted on a sample of 306 individuals from the Motivation Code database, generally corroborated these results. As Table 3 shows, all but one scale exhibited alphas above .70. The mean alpha was exactly the same at .80, again indicating strong overall internal consistency for Motivation Code.

Table 3

Motivation Code DATA SET 2: DATABASE VALIDATION STUDY

Alpha Range	No. of Scales in this Range
.60 to .69	1
.70 to .79	10
.80 to .89	16
Mean alpha of all 27 themes	0.80

Validity

The validity of an assessment provides an indication of the degree to which it measures the construct it is intended to measure. There are several types of validity. We address here content validity, two aspects

APPENDIX B: MOTIVATION CODE'S TECHNICAL DEVELOPMENT

of construct validity (factorial validity and convergent validity), and criterion validity.

CONTENT VALIDITY

Content validity refers to the degree to which an instrument adequately covers the content domain of the construct. There is no definitive taxonomy of motivational themes against which to compare Motivation Code. However, the SIMA foundation from which Motivation Code is derived provides strong evidence for content validity. Tens of thousands of SIMA biographies were analyzed to arrive at the SIMA taxonomy of recurring motivational themes. This provides strong evidence that the twenty-seven Motivation Code themes cover the content domain of motivation well.

CONSTRUCT: FACTORIAL VALIDITY

Construct validity is a broad term that refers to various indicators that a scale measures what it is intended to measure. There are several aspects to construct validity. Generally, the first aspect of construct validity to be addressed is known as factorial validity. This is evaluated through a statistical procedure known as factor analysis. Factor analysis provides an indication of the degree to which the items on a scale "hang together" and measure one, unified construct.

After we developed Motivation Code and demonstrated good overall reliability we conducted factor analyses on the two separate data sets shown in Tables 2 and 3. In the first data set, we conducted an exploratory factor analysis on each of the twenty-seven themes. All twenty-seven themes formed a single factor, indicating the items hang together well. All factor loadings (a statistic produced for each item that provides an indication of how well the underlying construct predicts the variance of that item) were above .30 (the conventional cutoff for an acceptable factor loading) except for one item. In fact, all factor loadings were above .40 except for three items. The average factor loading range across all twenty-seven themes was .54 to .70. These results provide strong support for the factorial validity of Motivation Code. They indicate that all twenty-seven themes measure a unified construct and that the items for each theme all measure the same concept.

CONSTRUCT: CONVERGENT VALIDITY

Convergent validity is exhibited when a measure correlates with other measures in theoretically predicted ways. For example, we would expect a measure of subjective well-being (social scientists' term for happiness) to correlate positively with a measure of self-esteem. People with high self-esteem generally experience more positive moods. If two such measures correlated negatively or not at all, that would suggest at least one of the measures is not measuring what it is supposed to measure.

In a first step to demonstrate convergent validity for Motivation Code, we correlated it with a short version of the Big-5 Personality Inventory. The Big-5 is one of the most widely used and scientifically robust measures of personality. It consists of five main factors, often presented using the acronym OCEAN: Openness, Conscientiousness, Extraversion, Agreeableness, and Neuroticism. These five personality factors are expected to overlap to some extent with many Motivation Code themes.

Examining the big picture of the 135 correlations, the results generally provide strong support for Motivation Code's validity. Most of the Motivation Code themes correlated in predicted directions (statistically significantly) with several of the Big-5 scales.

CRITERION VALIDITY

Criterion validity is an indication of the degree to which a scale predicts meaningful outcomes. We examined Motivation Code's criterion validity by investigating whether Motivation Code predicts the experience of flow and work performance. Flow refers to the experience of complete immersion in an activity, and it is often used to describe peak performance. Previous studies have confirmed the positive effects of flow on satisfaction and performance. In addition, there is evidence that flow plays a larger role in work activities compared with leisure activities. Although the preconditions for moving into a flow state have been identified (a balance between challenge presented and skill required for an activity), little is known about how these preconditions work in facilitating high performance. We tested the idea that using one's Motivation Code would mediate the relationship between flow experience and work performance.* Our results supported this theory, which also provides evidence for criterion validity, as an individual's motivation code predicts work performance in a theoretically predicted way.

CONCLUSION

Motivation Code is a new assessment of core motivation that utilizes a cutting-edge method that combines narrative and quantitative approaches. Motivation Code is currently being used in the areas of executive coaching and development, vocational development, team development, and employee engagement. Thus far, it has been used by corporations and faith-based organizations and it is rapidly expanding into new sectors. For these purposes, it has adequate reliability (internal consistency) and validity. The Motivation Code research team continues to expand the research base on validity and applied uses.

Motivation Code has been used to facilitate the development of individuals in numerous roles including: executive, student, teacher, manager, salesperson, and pastor. Motivation Code coach training is now being offered online and is currently being refined based on principles derived from positive psychology, narrative psychology, and the collective experience of current Motivation Code coaches.

---

* G. Lowe, T. W. Hall, D. C. Wang, and J. Miller, "Core Motivation: Bridging the Gap Between Flow Experience and Work Performance." Unpublished Dissertation, Biola University, La Mirada, CA, 2019.

Index

acceptance, 226
   Collaborate persons, 85
   Improve persons, 158
   Make the Grade persons, 91–92, 94
accountability
   Be Central persons, 200–201
   Organize persons, 146
   Serve persons, 102
achievement stories, identifying your, 20–22
Achieve Potential, 30–35
   aiming for the best, 30–31
   aversion to wasted potential, 31
   Frank's story, 5
   Sally's story, 30
   the shadow side, 31–32
   where they thrive, 34–35
   working with a person, 33–34
Achiever Family, 19, 51–82
   common characteristics of, 51
   four key themes of, 52–80
      Advance, 74–80
      Bring to Completion, 68–74
      Meet the Challenge, 52–60
      Overcome, 60–68
   summary of, 80–82

adding value, 156–57
Advance, 74–80
   four things a person might say, 78
   Kettering's story, 74–75
   problem-solving machines, 75
   process oriented, 75
   quick to act, 76
   resourcefulness, 76
   the shadow side, 76–78
   where they thrive, 80
   working with a person, 78–79
aiming for the best, 30–31
ambition, 66, 80, 81, 208
analysis paralysis, 119
analytical roles, 167
annoyance, 71
Apple, 188
asking for help, 72–73
asking questions, 118, 200
assertiveness, 188, 189
assessment. *See* Motivation Code assessment
assumptions, challenging, 138, 194
authoritarianism, 189–90

INDEX

bad behaviors, 101
barriers, 39, 62
Be Central, 197–201
   close to the action, 197
   critical to success of the team, 198
   eagerness to be called upon first, 197
   power hungry, 198
   the shadow side, 198–99
   three ways to engage, 199
   where they thrive, 201
   working with a person, 199–201
Be Unique, 192–97
   eagerness to be noticed, 193
   openness to new ways of thinking, 193–94
   the shadow side, 194–95
   sources of many ideas, 193
   where they thrive, 196–97
   willingness to take a stand, 193
   working with a person, 195–96
big picture, 58, 74, 129, 159
"blank sheet," 158
blind spots, 24
bonuses, 11
boredom
   Achieve Potential persons, 34–35
   Comprehend and Express persons, 117
   Demonstrate New Learning persons, 131
   Make It Work persons, 164–65
   Organize persons, 143
born performers, 183–84
bottlenecking, 144, 205–6
bottom line, 58–59
boundaries, establishing
   Bring Control persons, 191
   Experience the Ideal persons, 46
   Explore persons, 135, 136
   Gain Ownership persons, 205
   Overcome persons, 66
brainstorming, 90, 119–20, 134
Bring Control, 187–92
   assertiveness, 188
   bringing clarity, 189
   confidence boosters, 189
   driven to pull strings, 188
   the shadow side, 189–90
   where they thrive, 191–92
   working with a person, 190–91
Bring to Completion, 68–74
   arriving at the end result, 68–69
   Elizabeth's story, 68
   five non-work things for, 73
   getting caught up in momentum, 69
   process oriented, 69
   the shadow side, 70–71
   top producers, 69–70
   where they thrive, 73–74
   working with a person, 71–73
"brute force," 13
bucket lists, 139
burn out, 81, 224
   Be Central persons, 198
   Bring to Completion persons, 73

"can do" skills, 58
caught up in the momentum, 69
center of attention, 181. *See also* Be Central
   Evoke Recognition persons, 183, 184, 186–87
chain of command, 154
"change the world" roles, 46
chaos, 143, 192
clarity, 68, 189, 192
clean fuel, 225–27
clear "enemy," 67–68
closed-mindedness, 151
coaches
   Achieve Potential persons, 31
   Make an Impact persons, 36
codependent relationships, 199
Collaborate, 84–91
   author' story, 84
   eager for acceptance, 85
   Jason's story, 90
   relationship driven, 85
   the shadow side, 85–87
   unable to win unless the group wins, 84–85
   where they thrive, 89–91
   working with a person, 87–89

INDEX

combativeness, 64, 65
comfort zone, 59, 138, 195
commitment, to career, 129
common good, 66–67
communication roles, 109
compensation, 11–12
competency, 130
competitiveness
   Excel persons, 207, 208–9, 211
   Meet the Challenge persons, 54, 57–58
   Overcome persons, 62
complexity, 115, 116, 132, 312
Comprehend and Express, 114–21
   connecting the dots, 115
   eagerness to share learning, 114–15
   Lincoln's story, 114
   the shadow side, 115–18
   specialists, 115
   three ways to engage, 120
   where they thrive, 120–21
   working with a person, 118–20
confidence boosters, 189
confident leadership, 192
conflict
   Collaborate persons, 89
   Overcome persons, 63, 65
conflict avoidance, and Collaborate persons, 87
connecting the dots, 78, 115, 119, 121
consistency, 95
constant recognition, 184–85
construct validity, 240–42
contentment, 77
content validity, 241
context, and Advance persons, 79
continuous personal improvement, 47
contrarianism, 194
control. *See also* Bring Control
   Develop persons, 170
   Make an Impact persons, 39
   Organize persons, 144, 146
crafting your job, 221–22
creative industries, for Explore persons, 137–38
creative leadership roles, for Be Unique persons, 196

creative problem solvers, Make it Work persons, 163
credentials, 177
criterion validity, 243
cross-collaborative roles, 201
curiosity, 118, 134, 164

deadlines, 54, 71, 74, 75
Deci, Edward L., 11–12
defender of the code, 92–93
defining Motivation Code, 7–8
delegation, 171, 200
Demonstrate New Learning, 127–33
   Frank's story, 5
   generalists, 128–29
   Jim's story, 127–28
   quick learners, 128
   the shadow side, 129–30
   strong synthesizers, 129
   where they thrive, 132–33
   working with a person, 130–32
design roles, 173
detail-oriented
   Master persons, 122, 124, 126, 127
   Organize persons, 143
Develop, 167–73
   close involvement, 168–69
   Ella's story, 167–68
   highly practical, 169
   people person, 169
   process oriented, 168
   the shadow side, 169–70
   where they thrive, 172–73
   working with a person, 171–72
Die Empty (Henry), 221
diligence, 8–9, 123
directness, 39–40, 66, 177
dirty fuel, 225–27
discontentment, 80, 164, 168
dissatisfaction, 123–24, 136
distinctiveness, 195
dreams (dreaming), 32, 45, 48

Eagle Scouts, 91
early-stage work, 103, 177
embarrassment, 186

INDEX

emotional sensitivity, 118–19
empathy, 153, 176
   Develop persons, 169
   Establish persons, 176
   Influence Behavior persons, 105–6, 109
   Make It Right persons, 153
end results, 68–69
energy, 218–20
enjoying the present, 76
entertainers (entertainment)
   Evoke Recognition persons, 183–84, 187
   Influence Behavior persons, 109
entrepreneurs (entrepreneurship)
   Achieve Potential persons, 31
   Experience the Ideal persons, 41–42
   Organize persons, 143
Establish, 173–78
   assessing effectiveness of a plan, 175
   foundation layers, 174
   Jacob's story, 173
   seeing it through to the end, 175
   seeing the purpose, 174
   the shadow side, 175–76
   trustworthiness and reliability, 174–75
   wanting to be major factor, 174
   where they thrive, 177–78
   working with a person, 176–77
Evoke Recognition, 182–87
   born performers, 183–84
   drawn to the spotlight, 183
   excitement to receive attention for work, 183
   four ways to encourage a person, 185
   Kristie's story, 182
   the shadow side, 184–85
   where they thrive, 187
   working with a person, 186–87
Excel, 207–12
   ambitiousness, 208
   competitiveness, 207
   exceeding expectations, 207
   the shadow side, 208–9
   standard-bearers, 208
   where they thrive, 211–12
   working with a person, 210–11
exercises
   developing your Motivation Statement, 222
   identifying your achievement stories, 22
expectations
   Achieve Potential persons, 31–32
   Be Unique persons, 194
   Bring Control persons, 191
   Excel persons, 207, 210
   Make It Right persons, 152
   Meet the Challenge persons, 57
   Serve persons, 99
Experience the Ideal, 41–47
   bias to journey over destination, 41–42
   eagerness to attain perfect self, 42
   head in the clouds, 42
   Nick's story, 41
   the shadow side, 42–43
   where they thrive, 46–47
   working with a person, 44–46
Explore, 133–38
   crazy about novel experiences, 133
   idea generators, 134
   inspirational, 134–35
   Jill's story, 133
   the shadow side, 135–36
   where they thrive, 137–38
   willing to push the limit, 134
   working with a person, 136–37
"extrinsic" motivations, xi, 8, 12
eyes on the prize, 52, 55

factorial validity, 241
feedback
   Evoke Recognition persons, 184–85
   Improve persons, 159–60
   Influence Behavior persons, 105, 106
   Make It Right persons, 40
   Serve persons, 99
   talking about your motivation with manager, 222–24
Ferrell, Will, 207

flexibility, 12, 146
forest for the trees, 43, 70, 143, 147
Fortnite (video game), 52–53
forward momentum, 171
frustration, 42–43

Gain Ownership, 202–6
    Daniel's story, 202
    eagerness to acquire, 203
    goal focused, 203
    loyal protectors, 203
    masters of domain, 202
    the shadow side, 204–5
    stakeholders, 203–4
    where they thrive, 206
    working with a person, 205–6
generalists, 128–29, 132
generosity, 202
"get it done," 62, 71
"get to it" attitude, 31–32
goals
    Achiever Family, 81
    Gain Ownership persons, 203
    Make It Right persons, 153
    Meet the Challenge persons, 60
go-to people, 98
great unknowns, 40–41
group discussions, and Collaborate persons, 88
group projects, and Collaborate persons, 90

half-finished projects, 136–37, 175
hands-on, 170, 172
hard workers, 123
head in the clouds, 42
high-functioning teams, 89–90
high-growth organizations, 173
high stakes, and Meet the Challenge persons, 54
high standards
    Excel persons, 208, 209, 211
    Make it Right persons, 148–49, 150–51, 153
    Make the Grade persons, 92–93, 94, 95
    Serve persons, 98–99

hoarding, 204
hobbies, 139
honesty, 66, 89
Hopper, Grace, 161
hub roles, 201

idea generators, 134
"ideals," 44, 48
identity issues, 86, 88, 93
"I don't know if this is possible, but . . ." roles, 60
impatience, 38
impracticality, 116–17
Improve, 154–61
    adding value, 156–57
    Kevin's story, 154–55
    seeing the potential, 157
    the shadow side, 157–58
    things always being better, 155–56
    where they thrive, 160–61
    working with a person, 158–60
incentives, 10–11
indecisiveness, 116
independence, 86
individual identity, 86
individualistic bias, 95
inflexibility, 175
Influence Behavior, 104–10
    connecting with others, 105–6
    seeing the results of influence, 105
    the shadow side, 106–7
    Terri's story, 104–5
    where they thrive, 109–10
    working with a person, 107–8
innovation, 47, 121, 176, 193
inspirational, 134–35
instability, 131–32, 164
interpersonal development, 171–72
intimidation, 62, 105
intrepreneurs, Experience the Ideal persons, 41–42
"intrinsic" motivations, xi, 8, 12
introverts, 45
intuition, 42, 74, 76, 165
investigative roles, 167
Isaacson, Walter, 188

jack-of-all-trades, 129–30
job flexibility, 12
job retention, 14
job roles, 44–45
Jobs, Steve, 188
job satisfaction, 10–11
Jones, Ernest, 6
journey vs. destination, 61–62
juggling multiple tasks, 130–31

Kettering, Charles, 74–75
Key Contributor Family, 19, 181–213
   common characteristics of, 181
   six key themes of, 182–212
      Be Central, 197–201
      Be Unique, 192–97
      Bring Control, 187–92
      Evoke Recognition, 182–87
      Excel, 207–12
      Gain Ownership, 202–6
   summary of, 212–13
know-it-alls, 116, 130

laziness, 8–9
leadership
   Be Unique persons, 196
   Bring Control persons, 192
   Experience the Ideal persons, 42
   Gain Ownership persons, 206
   Make an Impact persons, 36
leaping first, 36
Learner Family, 19, 113–39
   common characteristics of, 113
   four key themes of, 113–38
      Comprehend and Express, 114–21
      Demonstrate New Learning, 127–33
      Explore, 133–38
      Master, 121–27
   summary of, 138–39
learning. *See also* Demonstrate New Learning; Learner Family
   Comprehend and Express persons, 114–15, 118
Lincoln, Abraham, 114

living out your motivation, 217–27
   crafting your job, 221–22
   looking for patterns, 220
   sources of energy, 218–20
lockers, 13
Lombardi, Vince, 209
"love to do" talents, 58
loyalty
   Establish persons, 174–75, 177
   Gain Ownership persons, 203
   Serve persons, 98

maintenance activities, 78, 170, 172
Make an Impact, 35–41
   ability to influence anything, 36
   eagerness to leap first, 36
   Joseph's story, 35–36
   the shadow side, 37–38
   against the status quo, 36
   where they thrive, 40–41
   working with a person, 38–40
Make It Right, 148–54
   devotion to clear standards, 148–49
   Parks's story, 148
   the shadow side, 149–51
   speaking up, 149
   strong moral compass, 149
   where they thrive, 153–54
   working with a person, 152–53
Make It Work, 161–67
   creativity, 163
   Hopper's story, 161
   natural fixers, 162
   practical minded, 162
   quick to move on, 162–63
   the shadow side, 163–64
   where they thrive, 166–67
   working with a person, 164–66
Make the Grade, 91–97
   attraction to groups with standards, 92
   awareness of what it takes, 91–92
   defender of the code, 92–93
   Scott's story, 91
   the shadow side, 93–94
   team oriented, 92

INDEX

where they thrive, 96–97
working with a person, 94–96
making a mountain out of a molehill, 65, 146, 163
manager, talking about your motivation with, 222–24
martyrs, 101
Master, 121–27
   detail-oriented, 122, 124, 126, 127
   hard workers, 123
   mastery over knowledge, 122
   Peart's story, 121
   perfectionism, 122
   the shadow side, 123–25
   top performers, 122–23
   where they thrive, 127
   working with a person, 125–26
masters of domain, 202
materialism, 204
"me against the world" attitude, 66–67
"means" vs. "ends," 77
meddling, 37, 100, 157
Meet the Challenge, 52–60
   author's story, 52–53
   competitiveness, 54
   fueled by high stakes, 54
   keeping eyes on the prize, 55
   relentlessly persistent, 53–54
   the shadow side, 55–57
   where they thrive, 59–60
   willing to pick up the slack, 55
   working with a person, 57–59
mentors, 30, 36
Miller, Arthur, Jr., x–xi
misunderstandings about motivation, 8–10
momentum, 14, 69, 79, 171
moon-shot initiatives, 40–41
moral compass, 149
motivation
   living out. *See* living out your motivation
   misunderstandings about, 8–10
   talking with manager about, 222–24
motivational families, 19
   the Achiever, 19, 51–81

the Key Contributor, 19, 181–213
The Learner, 19, 113–39
the Optimizer, 19, 141–79
the Team Player, 19, 83–111
the Visionary, 19, 29–49
motivational themes, 17–19. *See also specific themes*
Motivation Code
   benefits of managing with, 14
   defining, 7–8
   development, 237–38
   reliability, 238–40
   theoretical basis in contemporary psychology, 236–37
   validated foundation for, 234–35
   validity, 241–43
Motivation Code assessment, ix–xi, 19–25
   Frank's story, 4–5
   one step one: identifying your achievement stories, 20–22
   step four: discussing with a peer, 24–25
   step three: exploring the results, 23–24
   step two: taking the assessment, 22–23
Motivation Statement, 222

natural fixers, 162
nonconformity, 193, 194, 195–96
novel experiences, 133

obligations, 89, 103
"one size fits all," 13
open-ended projects and plans, 137, 164–65
optimism, 31–32, 33
Optimizer Family, 19, 141–79
   common characteristics of, 141
   six key themes of, 142–78
      Develop, 167–73
      Establish, 173–78
      Improve, 154–61
      Make It Right, 148–54
      Make It Work, 161–67
      Organize, 142–48
   summary of, 178–79

organizational development roles, 160
Organize, 142–48
    detail-oriented, 143
    entrepreneurialism, 143
    repulsed by chaos, 143
    the shadow side, 144–45
    signs a person stretched too thin, 146
    Tracy's story, 142
    where they thrive, 147–48
    working with a person, 145–47
Overcome, 60–68
    author's story, 60–61
    common enemies, 63–64
    journey over destination, 61–62
    not easily intimidated, 62
    perceptive of obstacles, 63
    the shadow side, 63–64
    unable to quit, 62
    where they thrive, 67–68
    working with a person, 65–67
overestimation, 209
overextended
    Be Central persons, 198
    Influence Behavior persons, 107, 110
    Organize persons, 144, 145
overthinking, 115–16
overvaluation, 106
overworking, 145

paralysis
    Achieve Potential persons, 33
    Comprehend and Express persons, 115–16, 119
    Improve persons, 158
Parks, Rosa, 148
passion, 41, 89, 221
patterns, looking for, 220
pay raises, 11
Peart, Neil, 121
Penner, Rod, ix–x
people persons, 160, 169
perceptive of obstacles, 63
perfectionism, 43, 122, 123–25, 126
"perfect job," 9–10
perks, 12
persistence, 53–54

personal distinction, 196–97
picking up the slack, 55, 93
point persons, 68, 109
positive spin, 32
possessiveness, 204
power hungry, 198
practicality, 72, 162, 169
praise, 11–12, 49, 186–87
problem-solvers, 75, 163
process oriented
    Advance persons, 75
    Bring to Completion persons, 69
    Develop persons, 168
    Make It Right persons, 154
    Make It Work persons, 164–65
    Organized persons, 148
procrastination, 56
productivity, 10–11
project management, 73–74, 147–48, 163
project roles, 160
promotions, 79, 126
public-facing roles, 187
pushing the limit, 134

question asking, 118, 200
quick learners, 128
quick to act, 76
quitting, 62, 129

"rationalization," 6
recognition. *See* Evoke Recognition
relational goals, of Make It Right persons, 153
relational issues, 165–66
relaxation, 64, 70
reliability, 174–75
remote working schedules, 12
research jobs, 119–20, 121, 138
resourcefulness, 76, 80, 163, 165
resources, 231–32
restlessness, 145, 164
reward structure, and Make The Grade persons, 96–97
rigidity, 175
risk-taking, and Meet the Challenge persons, 56

INDEX

role models, 108
routine tasks, as chores, 55–56
rule breakers, 135

satisfied employees, 10–11
self-awareness, 91–92, 108
self-care, 102
self-deprecation, 86
self-determination theory, 11–12
self-expression, 196
self-improvement, 75
selflessness, 99–100
self-possession, 67, 184
self-regulation, 108
Serve, 97–104
   caring for themselves, 100
   focusing on what's right, 99
   go-to people, 98
   great supporters, 98
   loyalty, 98
   Pam's story, 97
   quick to spot what is needed, 97–98
   the shadow side, 99–101
   where they thrive, 103–4
   willing to go above and beyond, 98–99
   working with a person, 101–3
shadow side
   Achieve Potential, 31–32
   Advance, 76–78
   Be Central, 198–99
   Be Unique, 194–95
   Bring Control, 189–90
   Bring to Completion, 70–71
   Collaborate, 85–87
   Comprehend and Express, 115–18
   Demonstrate New Learning, 129–30
   Develop, 169–70
   Evoke Recognition, 184–85
   Excel, 208–9
   Experience the Ideal, 42–43
   Explore, 135–36
   Gain Ownership, 204–5
   Improve, 157–58
   Influence Behavior, 106–7

Make an Impact, 37–38
Make It Right, 149–51
Make It Work, 163–64
Make the Grade, 93–94
Master, 123–25
Meet the Challenge, 55–57
Organize, 144–45
Overcome, 63–64
Serve, 99–101
sharing ideas, 117–18
short-term, easy wins, 59–60, 165, 179
side projects, 139
Smith, Will, 53–54
solo roles, 144
specialists, 115
spotlight-seekers, 181, 183, 184, 186–87. *See also* Be Central
spread too thin, 125–26
stakeholders, 203–4
standard-bearers, 153, 208
standards. *See* high standards
State of the American Workplace (2017 report), 10–11
status quo, 36, 134, 158
Steve Jobs (Isaacson), 188
stress levels
   Achiever persons, 81
   Make It Right persons, 150
   Meet the Challenge persons, 57
   Overcome persons, 63, 66
   Team Player Family, 110
submission to authority, 37, 41
substandard work, 79
swag, 96
synthesizers, 129
System For Identifying Motivated Abilities (SIMA), x–xi, 234–37

taking a stand, 193
taking on too much, 86
taking ownership, 179
Talladega Nights (movie), 207
targeted action plans, 59
teaching, 114–15, 118, 120, 132, 160
team cohesion, 14, 87, 92, 117

INDEX

Team Player Family, 19, 83–111
    common characteristics of, 83
    four key themes of, 84–110
        Collaborate, 84–91
        Influence Behavior, 104–10
        Make the Grade, 91–97
        Serve, 97–104
    summary of, 110–11
    three ways to nurture, 88
team recognition, 88, 90
tinkerers, 163–64
top producers, 69–70
trustworthiness, 174–75, 198
tunnel vision, 56–57, 71–72, 74
turnaround roles, 167

unhealthy competition, 208–9
uniqueness. *See* Be Unique
unrealistic expectations
    Achieve Potential persons, 31–32
    Be Unique persons, 194
    Bring Control persons, 191
    Excel persons, 210
    Make It Right persons, 152
    Meet the Challenge persons, 57
unwanted suggestions or advice, 157
upward mobility, 212

values, 94, 96, 110
visionaries, and Bring to Completion persons, 74
Visionary Family, 19, 29–49
    common characteristics of, 29
    summary of, 47–49
    three key themes of, 29–47
        Achieve Potential, 30–35
        Experience the Ideal, 41–47
        Make an Impact, 35–41

"white space," 158
win at all costs, 209
working for a cause, 91

www.ingramcontent.com/pod-product-compliance
Lightning Source LLC
Chambersburg PA
CBHW020338010526
44119CB00035B/449/J